CW01467513

MAN
OF
TWO
WORLDS

MAN
OF
TWO
WORLDS

My Life in Science Fiction and Comics

JULIUS SCHWARTZ
with Brian M. Thomsen

HarperEntertainment
An Imprint of HarperCollins*Publishers*

Frontispiece (top): The "Steuben Gang" in 1937. Kneeling, from left: Otto Binder, Manly Wade Wellman, and Julius Schwartz. Standing, from left: Jack Williamson, L. Sprague de Camp, John D. Clark, Frank Belknap Long, Mort Weisinger, Edmond Hamilton, and Otis Adelbert Kline. Frontispiece (bottom): The Dynamic Trio—Will Eisner, Julius Schwartz, and Bob Kane—reunited at the 1990 San Diego Comic Con.

All photographs and illustrations are from the personal collection of Julius Schwartz, except where indicated.
Justice League of America #56 © 2000 DC Comics.
Detective Comics #359 © 2000 DC Comics.
Superman #411 © 2000 DC Comics.
Action Comics #583 © 2000 DC Comics.
Strange Adventures #8 © 2000 DC Comics.
Atom #23 © 2000 DC Comics.
The Flash #163 © 2000 DC Comics.
The Flash #179 © 2000 DC Comics.
All rights reserved. Used with permission.

"Fer Chrisssakes, Schwartz, Get Outta My Face" by Harlan Ellison. Copyright © 1987 by The Kilimanjaro Corporation. Reprinted by arrangement with, and permission of, the Author and the Author's agent, Richard Curtis Associates, Inc., New York. All rights reserved.

MAN OF TWO WORLDS. Copyright © 2000 by Julius Schwartz and Brian M. Thomsen. All rights reserved. Printed in the United States of America. No part of this book may be used or reproduced in any manner whatsoever without written permission except in the case of brief quotations embodied in critical articles and reviews. For information address HarperCollins Publishers Inc., 10 East 53rd Street, New York, NY 10022.

HarperCollins books may be purchased for educational, business, or sales promotional use. For information please write: Special Markets Department, HarperCollins Publishers Inc., 10 East 53rd Street, New York, NY 10022.

FIRST EDITION
Designed by Joseph Rutt

Library of Congress Cataloging-in-Publication Data has been applied for.
ISBN 0-380-81051-4

00 01 02 03 04 ❖/RRD 10 9 8 7 6 5 4 3 2 1

For science fiction and comic book fans—
past, present, and future

ACKNOWLEDGMENTS

Special thanks to Allan Asherman, Paul Levitz, Bob Greenberger, Bob Wayne, Mike Carlin, Denny O'Neil, Mark Waid, Roy Thomas, Harlan Ellison, Ray Bradbury, David Drake, S. T. Joshi, Robert Madle, Charles N. Brown, Beth Gwinn, Ricia Mainhart, John Coker III, Liv Blumer, Tom Dupree, and Donna Benedetto Thomsen for their assistance.

CONTENTS

Contents

Contents

Contents

Stop!
Don't pass up this page!
My life (story) depends on it!

This is a memoir of my eighty-five years in science fiction and comics.

Now, eighty-five years is a long, long time, and some memories are clearer than others.

Remember—this is a memoir; it is the way *I* remember it.

Great minds are allowed to disagree and their recollections may differ from mine . . . and that's okay by me!

—*"Big Heart" Julie*

1998 SAN DIEGO COMIC CON

When I first agreed to work on this book with Julie, we concurred that it would probably be a good idea to attend a few comic book conventions together for a certain amount of atmospheric research.

Now, Julie and I had attended numerous science-fiction and fantasy conventions in the past (in the U.S. and abroad) and had even written bios for various program books for each other (his: "My Next Floor Neighbor—Brian Thomsen," mine: "What Becomes a Living Legend Most— Julius Schwartz), but it had been a while for both of us. I was now a freelancer sans expense account, and Julie—who as recently as six years ago had attended, on average, over twenty conventions a year—was slowing down just a bit, giving in to the occasional inconveniences of arthritis and other senior conditions.

I had never been to the San Diego Comic Con before, and an old friend of Julie's, John Broome (who had never been to *any* comic book convention before) was going to be there, so we girded our loins and set out cross-country for the convention.

As usual at these sorts of things, the convention hall was huge, and as luck usually has it, the area that was reserved for Julie to sit and sign autographs (with the various other senior luminaries of the comic book industry) was located at the opposite end of the hall from where we had entered.

"I'm going to take it slow," Julie informed me solemnly. "It's a long walk, and I may have to rest along the way."

"You're the boss," I replied. "You set the pace."

We figured we would walk to the DC booth—which was about halfway to our destination—rest, and then proceed. We weren't in any hurry. We would get there when we got there.

I paused a moment to look around, and Julie quickly darted from my side, going in the opposite direction from the one we had agreed upon.

"I'll be back in a moment," he relayed back. "I want to talk to Forry for a moment."

"Sure," I replied, recognizing Forrest J Ackerman, the famous fan and former editor of *Famous Monsters of Filmland* magazine, with whom Julie was now conversing.

A few minutes later we were back on our way to the halfway haven of the DC booth when we veered off in another direction as Julie saw Maggie Thompson of *Comic*

*With John Broome and Murphy Anderson at the 1998
San Diego Comic Con.* (DC Comics)

Buyer's Guide out of the corner of his eye, thus necessitating
another stop and gab. . . . And so it went, on a journey
across the hall with further stops to talk to Dave Stevens,
Mark Waid, Paul Levitz, and Stuart Moore as well as others
too numerous to mention or recall (as my memory is far
from being as sharp as that of Mr. Schwartz).

With each stop, Julie brightened; all fatigue and sense of
personal limitation had vanished.

When among old friends he was indefatigable.

Julie's autographing table was between Murphy Anderson
(of "Swanderson" fame and other myriad credits) and Paul S.
Newman (who was credited in *The Guinness Book of World
Records* as having written the most comic book scripts ever in
a career). But pretty much the entire rest of the comic universe funneled over there in the course of the weekend, a veritable who's who of comic books:

- Vince Sullivan, the editor who had originally bought the debut stories for both *Superman* and *Batman*, came by to talk over old times (shocking me with an anecdote about how he never met Bill Finger despite the fact that Finger had scripted most of the first *Batman* stories since, as far he was concerned, his deal was with Bob Kane, and Bill was just Bob's ghost scripter)
- Mike Richardson, publisher of Dark Horse Comics
- Will Eisner of *Spirit* fame
- Neal Adams, Denny O'Neil, Chris Claremont
- and John Broome, whom Julie had referred to as his best friend, his best writer, and his best man at his wedding. John had dropped out of comics decades ago and was currently living in Japan. He didn't really understand what all of the fuss was about at conventions (until he received a standing ovation from the audience at a panel that wanted to do nothing more than hear about his tenure as scripter on *The Atomic Knights*) and didn't make it back to the United States much since he, too, was just slightly getting on in years (like Julie) and was no longer as supple as a spring chicken.

(All of the above is, of course, in addition to the numerous adoring fans who paid good money for their convention memberships just for the opportunity to get a glance at the Living Legend himself.)

Sure, there were panels to attend, an awards ceremony, banquets, autographs to sign, and photos to pose for (usually with some attractive young person of the gentler sex like a Brinke Stevens or some other starlet), but there was always plenty of energy in the premier editor of DC's leading lines, the Living Legend himself.

By the end of the weekend I was exhausted, even though the only question anyone would ask me was, "So, when will the book be done?"

Julie, on the other hand, was looking forward to his next convention.

The indefatigable Schwartz was among friends and admirers, and all was right with the world.

—*Brian M. Thomsen*

MAN
OF
TWO
WORLDS

PART ONE

AT THE BEGINNINGS OF TIME

All of my life I have been punctual.

Everything I do has always been on the clock.

I never missed a deadline—better to be an hour early than a minute late—and on my tombstone will be the epitaph:

HERE LIES JULIUS SCHWARTZ
HE MET HIS LAST DEADLINE

I was always in the DC office by nine. I'd be a nervous wreck if the trains were late and I'd assure myself that it was positively not *my* fault.

Habitually, I'd count the number of steps from my house to the corner, to the subway, down the stairs, and up again . . .

and it was always higher mathematics if the escalator wasn't working: one . . . two . . . three . . . up to seventy.

Why, I even count the number of seconds it takes for a plane to lift off the runway at LaGuardia Airport, from the time it starts to accelerate up to the moment the plane safely leaves the terra firma (no more than thirty-two seconds, counted in elephants—one elephant, two elephants, etc.; others may use the four-syllable word "Mississippi," but my college professor preferred the word "elephant" as a counting device).

So you see, I've been a prisoner of time all my life.

I trace this obsession back to a momentous event early in my childhood, which provides me with a convenient spot to kick off the story of my life.

My parents, Joseph and Bertha, were of Jewish descent and emigrated from a small town outside Bucharest in Romania to come to the land of milk and honey—which other people have chosen to call the Bronx. My birth certificate indicates I was born at home: 817 Caldwell Avenue, the Bronx, and on June 19, 1915, I was enrolled in kindergarten at P.S. 5.

One morning while sipping my coffee out of a saucer, I looked at my parent's Big Ben clock, and, to my horror I realized that I was going to be late for promotion to the first grade—1-A, as it was called.

I bolted out of the house, dashed the two and a half blocks to P.S. 5 just as my classmates were marching into the new classroom. Heart pounding, I joined the tail end of the line . . . only to have the teacher pull me away from the others and order me back to the kindergarten room.

There I sat all alone, sobbing, shaking like a leaf, hardly able to breathe.

Eventually the teacher returned and informed me that I had been left back!

On that day I learned the terrible consequences of being *late!*

(Only recently have I come to understand what really happened that day. The decision to have me repeat kindergarten was automatic; it had nothing to do with my tardiness. Obviously my parents had enrolled me in school a semester too early. Accordingly, I had been kept back to put me on the proper schedule for my age group. And I nevertheless still managed to graduate high school at seventeen in 1932, a year earlier than others my age, thanks to skipping a couple of semesters.)

I was a library kid. It was my home away from home. I remember my first introduction to fantasy was a series of books called the *Blue Fairy* books (other colorful titles in the series included the *Red Fairy Book*, the *Yellow Fairy Book*, etc.), and at the time there wasn't really much else available in terms of fantasy or science fiction, unless you included the classics and other things that might be assigned in school.

Junior high put me in P.S. 45.

My best memory is of a short fellow student named Jules Garfinkel who appeared in a school play, delivering the melodic line "Swallow, swallow, little swallow" ever so sweetly. Years later he changed his name to John Garfield and carved out a short but successful career on Broadway and in Hollywood.

It was as a senior in Theodore Roosevelt High School that I gained my first editorial experience and (ahem) expertise. My mentor-to-be was a junior who edited the school publication called *The Square Deal*. As humor editor, I had a column called "Jest a Moment" (whose pun of a title I was quite proud of having come up with all by myself).

The editor of the weekly publication was a very talented fellow who showed me not only how to improve my own writing but also how to copyedit and proofread the works of others, as well. His name was Norman Cousins (actually his real name was *Cousin*, but since he was invariably addressed as *Cousins*, Norman eventually added the "s" as well), and he later went on to be the celebrated editor of *The Saturday Review*. He was the best editor I've ever known, and he taught me a lot about editing. I guess I owe him even more for introducing me to and breaking me into the field that would soon be my profession.

My entry in Senior Saga, *the 1932 Theodore Roosevelt High School yearbook.*

THE REAL FANTASTIC FOUR

Back when Mort Weisinger and I were in high school, attending another high school in the Bronx—DeWitt Clinton—were Bob Kane and Bill Finger, who were slated to cocreate *Batman*; Kane's classmate Will Eisner, who would go on to *Spirit* greatness; and a few years later, a youngster by the name of Stanley Martin Lieber, now known as Stan Lee.

So you see, during that time DeWitt Clinton High School was the home of the original Fantastic Four of comics.

Back in the Roaring Twenties, I was the world's biggest science fiction fan as well as the world's biggest Yankees fan (at least in my own mind). In those days it cost only a nickel to train ride to Yankee Stadium from where I lived, and fifty cents for a seat in the bleachers. I preferred to sit behind right field—dubbed "Ruthville"—to be close to my idol, Babe Ruth, the Big Bambino.

I'd have recurring dreams about Babe Ruth, nightmare fantasies in which he'd hit a ball so high and far that an outfielder would go up after it in a flying machine holding a butterfly net. He'd swoop in on it and snare it, robbing Ruth of a home run.

(Come to think of it, I wish I'd have used that as a plot gimmick when I edited *Strange Sports Stories*!)

I was once having a conversation with Dark Horse Comics publisher and rabid Yankees fan "Big" Mike Richardson, when the question came up as to why Yankee

Stadium is called the House that Ruth built.

"You know why?" I quizzed

Mike replied questioningly, "Because he was such a big draw?"

"Partially right, but mostly wrong," I hit back.

"Around 1919, when Ruth was a pitcher for the Boston Red Sox, he held the World Series record for pitching consecutive scoreless innings. When not on the mound, he'd play outfield so Boston could take advantage of his big bat. Boston then sold him to the Yankees for big bucks (thus allegedly bringing down the curse of the Bambino on Boston that has deprived them of a Pennant ever since!).

"The American League Yankees used to play their home games at the Polo Grounds, home turf of the National League New York Giants. It bugged John McGraw, legendary manager of the Giants, that the Ruth-playing Yankees proved more of a draw than his home team. So he snapped, 'I'm not letting the Yankees play here anymore! Let Ruth build 'em their own ballpark!'

"And that's exactly what 'he' did!"

The "Sultan of Swat" signed a contract with the Yankees in 1927 for a record eighty thousand dollars, making him the highest-paid baseball player. He was asked to justify his eighty grand when at the time Herbert Hoover, the president of the United States, was only making seventy-five thousand dollars.

Ruth snapped back, "I had a better year than Hoover! Besides, how many home runs did Hoover hit last year?"

Before there were night games in the ballparks, before lights and domes and giveaway stuff, if a game was rained out, it had to be made up with a doubleheader, usually on a Sunday, always on a July Fourth or Labor Day, to draw a sellout crowd. The second game lasted past 7 o'clock.

I used to live about a half hour from Yankee stadium. So at about 6:30 on Sundays, I'd bolt out of the ballpark, even before the game was over, to get home no later than seven o'clock. Why? Because Jack Benny was on the radio Sunday nights at seven, and not even my beloved Yankees could stop me from getting my Jack Benny fix!

Many years later, my wife and I went to the Westbury Music Fair on Long Island to see Jack Benny in person (a young Wayne Newton was his opening act). It is a theater-in-the-round, and at the intermission as Benny was going up the stairs past us, my wife stopped him and got him to autograph the program book. It turned out to be my birthday present!

In the late 1920s, I devoured dime novels (then costing fifteen cents). I especially liked Dick and Frank Merriwell sports stories and Nick Carter detective mysteries—I preferred those featuring the villain Dr. Quartz because his name sounded so much like my name.

Then one day, fresh out of reading material, I got my friend Charlie Whalen to trade a couple of paperbacks for a big (really big) magazine, *Amazing Stories*.

The cover illustration of that June 1926 issue was signed "Paul" and featured a giant sea serpent coming up out of the ocean, threatening three guys on a raft. It was the cover illustration for the second installment of *A Journey to the Center of the Earth* by Jules Verne. (Note: Verne, in the text of the story, apologizes to the reader for not being able to sufficiently describe the scene in question; Paul didn't have any problem with it.)

I devoured that issue, cover to cover. There was "The Star" by Verne's old rival H. G. Wells as well as yarns by G. Peyton Wertenbaker, Otis Adelbert Kline, and Charles W. Wolfe. But the story that literally hooked me was "The Runaway Skyscraper" by Murray Leinster, with an opening line that sucked me right in:

> The whole thing started when the clock on the Metropolitan Tower began to run backwards.

And from that day on I was hooked! This was infinitely better than the *Blue Fairy* books back at the library!

AMAZING STORIES

I consider March 5, 1926, to be the most important day in science fiction history. That was the date <u>Amazing Stories</u> first appeared on the newsstand. It was the first all-science-fiction magazine, mostly reprints of writers like H. G. Wells, Jules Verne, and Edgar Allan Poe. (Very little science fiction was written back then; there was no market for it. The only magazines occasionally printing science fiction were <u>Weird Tales, Blue Book</u>, and <u>Argosy</u>, which tagged them "Different Stories.")

The other thing about <u>Amazing Stories</u> that made an

impression on me (besides its wondrous contents) was the name on the cover: "Hugo Gernsback, Editor." Imagine that! This was the man who was in charge of everything! Like a general in charge of his troops, it fell to him to make all of the decisions of the magazine. It was as if he was some god from the heavens who descended onto Earth to bring forth this wonderful magazine!

One day I came across a letter in an SF Reader's column in *Amazing Stories*—or perhaps it was *Science Wonder Stories*—from a Mortimer Weisinger, telling about a club in the Bronx called the Scienceers and inviting anyone who was interested in joining to write him for further information.

I immediately sent off my hopeful penny postcard—and just as immediately was heartbroken to find that I couldn't join the club yet since it had a strict rule that you had to be at least sixteen years of age before you could become a member.

Impatiently, I waited a month until I qualified, and then on my sixteenth birthday I sent a card saying that I was ready to join. I got an answer back inviting me to the next meeting, which was to be held in the basement of Mortimer Weisinger's home. Not having the nickel trolley fare, I walked—make that jogged—the couple of miles across town to where the meeting was being held on a day that would be a turning point in my life.

Just as I got there, several guys came storming out of the basement, all of them grumbling about something or other.

I ventured into the basement to find out what was going on. There I met the lone remaining Scienceer still there: Mortimer Weisinger.

I introduced myself, told him that I was there to join the Scienceers, and asked what had just happened and where was the rest of the club.

Mort explained that he was the club's treasurer and had just reported that there was temporarily no money in the treasury because he had squandered it all on SF magazines, candy, and the movies.

With nothing else to do, Mort and I hung out and talked and kept talking for hours about science fiction . . . which, after all, had been the real reason I had journeyed across town to begin with.

Had the meeting been held without a hitch (and with full attendance), Mort and I might never have had the opportunity to bond with each other. And who knows? I might not have enjoyed the meeting and as a result might never have entered fandom.

We became fast friends and would often meet halfway at a public library and talk and talk about the science fiction stories we read and who our favorite writers were. From

The Scienceers!
Mort—second row, far right;
me—top row, center

time to time we used to play challenge games, trying to stump each other with questions about science fiction. We considered ourselves two of the foremost experts on science fiction in 1931, and to the best of our knowledge, no one disputed our assertion.

We especially loved the stories written by David H. Keller, M.D. the most popular science-fiction writer of the time. We wondered: *Who is Dr. Keller? What does the "H" stand for? Where does he live? What kind of doctor is he? What new stories does he have in the works?*

DAVID H. KELLER, M.D.

(an excerpt from an article/interview from the July 1933 issue of *Science Fiction Digest* by Julius Schwartz and Mortimer Weisinger)

Dr. David H. Keller was born in Philadelphia in 1880 and received his M.D. in 1903. For many years he was a country doctor, and then in 1914 he began what he terms his Odyssey, in which he traveled far and saw much. He went into the World War as a First Lieutenant and at present is a Lieutenant-Colonel in the Medical Reserves. . . .

He has been writing since the age of 14. "We learn to do by doing," he explained, "and I suppose I learned to write by writing. I wrote thirteen novels and over fifty stories before I tried to sell any one of them. Then my wife said I must try to write for profit and I wrote and sent "The Revolt of the Pedestrians" to <u>Amazing Stories</u>. Hugo Gernsback seemed to like it, and sent me a contract for ten more stories at forty dollars each. Before I accepted this he raised the offer to sixty dollars each. That seemed a lot of money, but the real pleasure came in seeing the first story in print.

(Dr. Keller had a name for his beautiful home "Underwood"—named after the typewriter whose technical support in conjunction with his own creative output had financed its purchase. He even invited me for the weekend once to come visit, and meet his family in Steubenville, Ohio. Mort was terribly jealous when I told him about my coup. It was no secret that the good doctor preferred my company to Mort's. My good friend in fandom just couldn't accept that Dr. Keller had singled me out. The esteemed author took me to breakfast at the Hotel New Yorker (it was the first time I had ever eaten in a restaurant). When the time of my trip came, I triumphantly strode to Penn Station and boarded the train . . . only to be met at disembarkment by Mort who, not wanting to miss out on my treat, had hitchhiked all the way from the city to horn in on my exclusive. I could have killed him!)

Almost simultaneously it occurred to us that it would be a nifty idea to share our newfound knowledge with others. Wouldn't it be great if we told our fellow fans about these writers, what stories they were working on, what new stories they had coming up? We drafted several letters and sent them off to the science fiction magazines asking that the correspondence be forwarded to the authors.

Soon responses started coming in. The first was from Edward E. Smith, Ph.D., author of the popular story "The Skylark of Space." We began to compile the answers to our questions. The problem was that we really didn't know what to do with the information now that we had it. I recalled the Judy Garland and Mickey Rooney movies and how they would always solve their problems by "putting on a show," so I suggested we do the same in the form of a fan magazine.

Mort and I were sixteen-plus years old and didn't feel professional enough to put on a "show"—in our case a *real* magazine—on our own, so we persuaded the rest of the Scienceers to get back together and cooperate in putting out a mimeographed magazine similar to the club's bulletin, which had been previously christened *The Planet.*

The title of our first effort was *my* idea. It was called *The Time Traveller* (inspired by the English spelling of the name of the main character in H. G. Wells's novel *The Time Machine).* Lacking confidence in our own editorial abilities, we asked Allen Glasser, the Scienceers' president and editor of *The Planet* (and a prominent "letterhack" who even pre-dated Forrest J Ackerman in fandom) to be the editor. I was managing editor, and Mort was associate editor (the two of us shared the staff box with Ackerman as contributors). When completed, *The Time Traveller* consisted of six pages,

THE TIME TRAVELLER

Science Fiction's Only Fan Magazine

Volume 1 No. 6 JULY, 1932.	**ALLEN GLASSER** EDITOR	10 Cents per Copy $1 per Year
MORTIMER WEISINGER Associate Editor	JULIUS SCHWARTZ Managing Editor	FORREST J. ACKERMAN Contributing Editor

The masthead for an issue of The Time Traveller.

with Glasser stenciling the first two, me the next two, and Mort the final two.

The premier issue was dated January 1932, and made its debut on January 9 as *The Time Traveller—"Science Fiction's Only Fan Magazine."* It featured a biography of Captain S. P. Meek (as part of what we hoped would be an ongoing science fiction who's who column), a brief interview with Bob Olsen, a list of scientifilms films (by Ackerman), the first installment of "The History of Science Fiction" (by Weisinger), a science-fiction contest, an article giving the inside dope on Otis Adelbert Kline's "The Planet of Peril," and a description of a visit to the offices of *Weird Tales* by letter hack Jack Darrow, along with news items about authors and their forthcoming stories.

We sent off subscription notices to the various names and addresses we found in the letter columns of the science fiction magazines like *Amazing Stories.* We sold future issues for a dime each and became the first nationally distributed science-fiction fanzine. We netted about thirty subscriptions at the special rate of twelve issues for a dollar.

THE BIG BANG THEORY OF
THE CREATION OF SUPERMAN

Among The Time Traveller's first subscribers was a fellow named Jerome Siegel from Cleveland. So enthusiastic was he about the magazine that it inspired him to put out one of his own. It was called Science Fiction and it featured fiction stories rather than articles. Not having any money to print it, he got permission to use the mimeograph in his high school.

Jerry's main ambition was to make it as a big-time science-fiction writer and sell his stories to the pulps. He wanted to be as good and popular a writer as his idol, Edgar Rice Burroughs. Reserving his real name for future, more polished stories, Siegel used pseudonyms on his early self-published yarns. (After all, he rationalized, Edgar Rice Burroughs used the pen name Normal—mistakenly printed as "Norman"—Bean for his first published story!)

For the January 1933 issue of Science Fiction, Siegel whipped up and featured one of his stories entitled "The Reign of the Superman" under the pen name of Herbert S. Fine ("Herbert" from the first name of a cousin, "S. Fine" from his mother's maiden name).

The Superman featured in the title of the story was a villain and later discarded for a hero in a follow-up version. (A minor character was named "Forrest Ackerman.")

Thus I theorize that if Mort and I had not created our fanzine, neither would have Jerry Siegel created his—and as a result may never have triggered his creation of the original Living Legend, Superman. No Siegel fanzine, no Siegel Superman!

And that's my "Big Bang Theory" about the creation of Superman.

Within two issues the crude mimeographed 'zine evolved into a typeset magazine, thanks to a fellow fan by the name of Conrad Ruppert who owned some typesetting equipment and offered to print the magazine for us for little more than the price of the paper.

In addition to the information we had gathered from our questionnaires (and investigative digging into the identity of some major authors who were writing under various different pseudonyms), the magazine featured reviews, gossip columns, bibliographies, science articles, and, occasionally, fiction.

A monumental coup of ours was an exciting eighteen-part "round robin" serial *Cosmos*, which ran from the July 1933 issue (now called *Science Fiction Digest*) through the October/November 1934 issue (now retitled *Fantasy Magazine*), featuring chapters by such majors authors of that day as A. Merritt, Otto Binder, E. E. "Doc" Smith, Ralph Milne Farley, David H. Keller, John W. Campbell, and Edmond Hamilton—a veritable science-fiction who's who of the time.

The January 1930 premier issue of *Astounding Stories of Super Science* listed Harry Bates as editor, a name unfamiliar to science fiction fandom at the time. The magazine became the number-one market for science fiction because Bates was paying two cents a word on acceptance, whereas the competition's rate was a half cent a word payable on publication. Needless to say, he had first choice on the cream of the crop.

I remember the first time I cast my eyes on *Astounding*.

It was love at first sight!

I needed to know what the weather was going to be (hoping for snow that would be perfect for sledding). Back in those days—before cable TV's Weather Channel and radio's all-weather stations—if you wanted to know what the weather was going to be in the quickest and fastest way possible (beyond looking out your window at the weather of the moment), you would go down to the local newsstand and check out the latest edition newspaper for the weather forecast. Which I did—and there was *Astounding*, distracting me from my meteorological research. A new science-fiction magazine—Issue #1, January 1930! I had to have it! I rushed back home and begged my mother for the princely sum of twenty cents to satisfy my need. *Astounding* and I were a match made in heaven!

Mort and I loved going up to the editorial offices of the various science-fiction magazines and getting the "hot news" on forthcoming issues. We were always in awe of the editors. To us, they were the closest things to gods on Earth.

On one occasion while interviewing editor Harry Bates, the earthbound god turned the tables and started to interview me, inquiring what were my favorite stories from *Astounding*. I quickly thought about it and replied, "The ones about the space pirate Hawk Carse by Anthony Gilmore," then immediately jumped at the opportunity to add, "and I'd really like to know more about him."

Harry Bates smiled and revealed that there really wasn't anyone named Anthony Gilmore. It was the collaborative pseudonym of two science fiction writers, and he hastened to add that he wasn't free to reveal their true identities.

When I published the scoop in *Science Fiction Digest*, guesses bounced back and forth for months as debate raged on concerning the authors' real identities—all denied by Bates. Eventually by comparing styles, I deduced that "Anthony Gilmore" was in reality Harry Bates and his assistant editor, Desmond Hall. The two of them were selling stories to themselves!

When *Astounding* was eventually sold to Street & Smith, Harry Bates began writing stories under his own name. One of these stories was the classic and truly outstanding "Farewell to the Master," which was eventually made into the movie *The Day the Earth Stood Still*.

HARRY BATES

(From an article/interview by Julius Schwartz and
Mortimer Weisinger in Science Fiction Digest, February 1933.)

Harry Bates was editor of the popular Clayton magazines Astounding Stories and Strange Tales. Was born in Pennsylvania thirty-two years ago, but he looks twenty-six. Is a very congenial, likeable chap and a regular fellow and not a dignified old graybeard as is imagined by his fans. . . .

Acquired his taste for science fiction at an early age. He has done very little reading of contemporary science fiction. He is kept posted on the movements of rivals by his authors. The first story he accepted for Astounding was Ray Cummings's "Phantoms of Reality." It wasn't a good story, and he knew it.

Bates expresses little hope for the reappearance of Astounding Stories. Explains that Astounding started about two months before the stock market crash. The circulation rose slowly but definitely until the last six months, when it suddenly zoomed down, deeming it inadvisable to continue publishing the magazine since the lucrative returns did not compensate the risk and energy put into it. . . .

(Note: Despite Bates's dire assessment of the situation Astounding Tales of Super Science survived the Depression, and is still published today under the title of Analog Science Fiction/Science Fact.)

One summer day in 1934 I went hiking in Palisades Park with Mort and another friend, Otto Binder (who later scripted more than five hundred Captain Marvel stories), when—BAM!—a car hit us and knocked us over like a row of ten pins. Sometime later we came to in the hospital.

We were very lucky, and I often wonder what might have been different in science fiction and comics had we been wiped out on that day upstate. . . . But, fortunately, I guess it just wasn't our time.

Not too soon after, Mort hit me with an idea. As long as we were so familiar with the field's writers (we *were* experts, after all) and were frequently going to the editors' offices looking for news, we might as well take a crack at making a living from it.

We knew the editors quite well from asking them for information on this and that and were almost on a friendly basis with them. We knew the science-fiction field, as limited as it was in those days, and we decided to contact a number of the authors we corresponded with, suggesting that they send their stories directly to us, thus saving them the long time of waiting on editors' desks and the back-and-forth postage as their manuscripts made their editorial rounds. We would act as their agents, get quick editorial decisions and checks, keeping ten percent of whatever we got them as our fee. And thus Solar Sales Service was born—as well as my career as a science-fiction professional.

PART TWO

SCIENCE FICTION: FROM FANDOM TO BUSINESS

One day, Isadore Manson, a fellow Scienceer, showed me a story in the April 1929 issue of *Munsey's Magazine* called "The Heat Wave" by M. Ryan and R. Ord. I started to read it . . . and I was shocked!

The story read almost word for word the same as "Across the Ages," a story by Allen Glasser, my fellow editor of *The Time Traveller* that had appeared in the August 1933 *Amazing Stories.* I still recall the last line of the original in *Munsey's:* "He stared at her with horror in his eyes." Glasser's *Amazing* version read: "He stared at her with dawning horror in his eyes."

Glasser had made a few other improvements, but it was still a literary crime, plagiarism, and I had to report it.

I bolted to the Manhattan editorial offices of *Amazing* at 222 West 39th Street and told the editor, Dr. T. O'Connor Sloane, what I had discovered, thus cutting short Allen's brief career as a science-fiction writer.

DR. T. O'CONNOR SLOANE

Thomas O'Connor Sloane was born in 1851, went to St. Francis Xavier College and Columbia University and served as a professor of natural sciences at Seton Hall College during the late nineteenth century. He invented a piece of equipment called a self-recording photometer and designed a new method of determining the sulfur content of illuminating gas.

He was a prominent inventor and a great grey eminence . . . and in the early thirties he was the editor of <u>Amazing Stories</u>.

At the time I was a literary agent selling him stories about space warps and light speed and interplanetary travel, and he was buying them for publication, but I still vividly remember him assuring me, "Space travel can't work, you know."

Here was a scientist, a man who had already seen over eighty years of scientific and technological advancement, an arbiter of taste for one of the major science-fiction magazines—indeed, one of the gods on earth—and in his old man's cynicism, he still intimated that he just didn't buy into the magic of the future . . . which, of course, never interfered with his decision to buy stories that contradicted his beliefs.

After all, business was business. (He had a placard on his desk with a line from the song "Old Man River" that read, I'M TIRED OF LIVIN' AND 'FRAID OF DYING.)

Dr. Sloane seemed to like me quite a bit after that (or maybe he just suffered my presence just a little more readily). When he'd give me an advance copy of *Amazing Stories* magazine, I would sit in the subway on the way back home to the Bronx, proudly holding up next month's issue for everyone to notice (or not, as the case usually was).

Just imagine! I had a copy that had not yet appeared on the newsstand! A metaphoric gift from one of the gods himself.

Little did my fellow straphangers realize that among them was someone special, a figurative time-traveler reading a magazine of the future in the present-day.

Here were Mort and I, in touch with the editors of all the professional science-fiction magazines in the world. I personally knew the men behind not only *Amazing Stories* but *Wonder Stories* and *Astounding*, as well. They were my idols!

Once in a while Dr. Sloane (or F. Orlin Tremaine of *Astounding* or Charles D. Hornig of *Wonder Stories*) would say something like, "I wish I had a short time-travel story to fill a hole in next month's issue." And with a heavy sigh he would tackle the slush pile (unsolicited manuscripts), looking for something to fill the hole.

Here was someone sighing over a task that I would have given my right arm to do, occasionally venting frustration over not having the right story to fix the editorial mix for a given issue. It was pretty hard to sympathize with him.

Mort pointed out to me, "The writers don't know what these editors need at the time when they need it. They just bang out their stories . . . and then blindly submit them, running the risk that while their story is sitting on one desk, a hole in an issue of another magazine is waiting to be filled by a story just like theirs—provided they get around to submitting there before that hole gets filled. They just sit at their typewriters turning out stuff, hoping that they are in the right place at the right time."

"Aha! I get it!" I cut in. "What they really need is an agent to tip them off as to who wants what!"

"To make sure that they are in the right place at the right time."

"Exactly!" I agreed.

We were still not yet out of our teens, but that didn't stop us from teaming up as the first literary agents specializing in science fiction and fantasy. Thus was formed Solar Sales Service (oh, how we loved that alliteration!), and we set out to set the world of magazine publishing on fire.

After making our rounds of the editorial offices we sent out letters to every science-fiction writer whose address we had advising them:

[We have] made an extensive survey of the entire science-fiction field through a series of talks with the various editors, and as a result [are] firmly convinced that fantasy fiction is due for a renaissance. . . .

We then outlined the general needs of each of the publications and editors and set forth the terms of our intended arrangement:

As for our terms, they are extremely reasonable. We ask only that all stories sent us be accompanied with a dollar sales service fee. This fee is waived just as soon as we sell three stories for the client. Of course, we ask the usual 10 percent commission on all American sales, 15% on English sales. . . .

We followed the statement of our intended terms with glowing recommendations that we had solicited from Sloane, Hornig, and other editors in the field with whom we had made contact. (They realized the advantage of using us as a preliminary screen of the materials because we knew what they wanted and would vouch for its quality. Besides, it was better than spending so much time searching through the great unknown of the slush pile.)

Our first submission came from Edmond Hamilton, a well-known science-fiction writer from New Castle, Pennsylvania, whose published stories we had enjoyed reading. The 7,000-word story was titled "Master of the Genes," and clipped to the manuscript was a dollar bill—our very first reading fee!

Mort and I opened the envelope, excited about its contents, and looked at the dollar bill, then at each other. We broke out in laughter.

For years we had bought magazines to read Hamilton's

stories, literally paid for the privilege, and now he was paying us a dollar to read a new one! We sent the dollar back—followed later with a note containing the news that *Wonder Stories* had accepted the story for thirty-five dollars (1/2 cent per word).

Splitting our ten percent commission meant that Mort and I each took home a dollar and seventy-five cents apiece.

We were on our way!

Where? We had no idea. All we knew was that the more we hobnobbed with the editors and writers, the better our agency would do.

Only time would tell where we would wind up!

I remember one incident with F. Orlin Tremaine, then editor of *Astounding*. After checking out the competition he had read in the current issue of *Wonder Stories*—which included a story that would eventually be recognized as one of the ten greatest science-fiction stories of all time, namely "A Martian Odyssey" by Stanley G. Weinbaum—Tremaine told me that any Weinbaum story I submitted to him would be a surefire sale to *Astounding* at the top pay scale available: a penny a word on acceptance!

What a deal! Just imagine it—I would be Weinbaum's agent!

The only problem was how to pull it off.

I didn't know Weinbaum. Who was Weinbaum? Where was Weinbaum?

Where did I start my quest?

Just then inspiration struck.

I remembered that my old friend Charlie Hornig (in addition to being the editor to whom I had sold Hamilton's "Master of the Genes," Charlie was also my second best friend in the world—after Mort, of course) was the editor of *Wonder Stories* (*Astounding*'s competitor), where "A Martian Odyssey" had originally appeared. So I bolted over to his office hoping to come up with a plan to finagle the information out of him.

I told Charlie that I had heard that "Weinbaum" was actually the pseudonym for another well-established writer who was trying to double his sales. Charlie was skeptical and didn't believe me, but I pressed on, telling him to check the address Weinbaum used. Maybe we would recognize it and uncover his real identity.

Charlie looked it up and said it was Milwaukee.

What a break for me! Science-fiction writer Ralph Milne Farley lived in Milwaukee, was the author of the popular "Radio Planet" stories—and was really a pseudonym for Roger Sherman Hoar, an attorney.

I nodded my head and asked innocently, while he still had the Weinbaum file at hand, "What street address did he use? Maybe it's Ralph Milne Farley?" Charlie told me without giving it a second thought to prove it wasn't Farley.

I nodded again, making a quick mental note of it, and quickly made a fast exit from the Gernsback offices, making up some other commitment as an explanation to allay any suspicions.

No sooner was I out the door than I jotted down Stanley Weinbaum's address.

I dashed off a letter to Weinbaum via the address Charlie had unwittingly provided, advising him that I had an "in" with a sure market for him that would pay him a penny a word on acceptance, twice the rate that *Wonder Stories* was paying him on publication!

Weinbaum sent me "Flight on Titan," which I sold for $92, soon followed by "Parasite Planet" for $125, and "The Lotus Eaters" for $120. Three out of three! Talk about batting a thousand!

I sold his next fifteen stories, as well. I sold them all.

So prolific was he that he once had two stories in the same issue of *Astounding*, the second ("The Adaptive Ultimate") under the name of John Jessel (his grandfather's name).

Unfortunately bad news soon arrived.

Stan came down with throat cancer and died at the too-young age of thirty-three. The cancer was first spotted by Dr. Eugene Kaye, a friend in Milwaukee (with whom Weinbaum and his wife, Marge, often double-dated). It was Eugene Kaye who noticed while they were out one night that Stan was suffering from a shortness of breath. Stan dismissed it but claimed to be bothered by a sore throat. The good doctor took a look and made an appointment to examine him and X-ray his throat in order to check it out. The result: cancer . . . and Stanley Weinbaum was dead within a few months.

Dr. Kaye later went on to marry Mrs. Weinbaum (who kept on signing her correspondences with Stanley's agent and editors as "Stan's Marge").

On one occasion when I complimented the legendary Isaac Asimov on having his story "Nightfall" selected by the

Science Fiction Writers of America as the best science-fiction story of all time, he shook his head and asserted that that honor rightfully belonged to Stanley Weinbaum's "A Martian Odyssey." It was the first story that treated aliens as aliens. (It is also one of the stories included in the landmark anthology edited by Donald A. Wollheim entitled *The Pocket Book of Science Fiction* [Pocket Books, 1943].)

STANLEY G. WEINBAUM

Though unquestionably Weinbaum was the top writer in the field at the time, the status of the pulp industry and its practices often made it difficult for one to actually collect one's pay for a given story unless you actually had someone in place to hound them or demand a check on acceptance or on pub. According to Stanley's widow, he never was paid for his classic "A Martian Odyssey" (which I, regretfully, did not represent).

At one point Weinbaum was considering suing his publisher, Hugo Gernsback of *Wonder Stories* for payment.

I offered him some advice in a letter dated June 24, 1935:

. . . Regarding suing Wonder—now we're in a pickle. You can sue and collect, but what would be the chances of making future sales there? Now that you have the $25 per 6000 word story agreement, do you think it would be the wisest thing to do? In other words: either sue Wonder for the dough they owe you, and forget about future sales there, or hope they'll pay you eventually, and in the meantime [keep]

> getting the $25 on acceptance of new stories. . . .
> Send your stories to me as usual and I will
> personally deliver them to <u>Wonder</u>. If they're rejected,
> they will be returned to me (and I can submit them
> elsewhere). If they're accepted you'll be notified, and
> the check will be sent to you. You can then send me
> back my ten percent commission on the deal. . . .
>
> And as a result Weinbaum was paid regularly for those
> stories that were handled through me, showing the
> advantage even then of having a conscientious and,
> "ahem," tough literary agent.

The magazine business wasn't just rough on writers. Competition was tough on the newsstands, as well, causing the death of many a title.

Wonder went under, and Gernsback sold it to Standard Magazines, who would publish it with a new title: *Thrilling Wonder Stories*. When Mort got wind of the new magazine, he quickly darted over to Leo Marguiles and inquired who was going to edit it. (Being an agent had been neat, but it didn't rank anything next to actually being one of the gods on Earth—or at least so Mort thought.)

The likely candidate was Charlie Hornig, since he had helmed *Wonder.*

Not one to pass on self-interest in deference to friendship, Mort quickly pointed out that that was probably not really a great idea. After all, if Charlie had done such a wonderful job at *Wonder*, why had it failed?

The point was considered; then the young agent-editor was asked who he thought might make a better candidate.

The ever-humble Mort didn't tarry for a second and recommended himself—and he was quickly hired to the editorial posting.

Before he became an editor, John W. Campbell wrote science fiction of the type that is now known as "hard science fiction" (as pioneered by Doc Smith of "Skylark" and "Lensman" fame), but he wanted to broaden his market potential.

After several "thrilling wonder" rejections from Mort (who had by this time quit Solar Sales Services and was safely ensconced as an editor for Standard magazines), Campbell called upon Mort for an explanation.

Mort explained that Campbell was writing stories that were too loaded with science for his younger *Thrilling Wonder* readers. He advised him to get into the story action faster, load it up with adventure and thrills, and ditch all of the hardcore science facts.

Mort Weisinger and John W. Campbell.

Campbell asked him to recommend an author to model his stories after and use as an example of *Thrilling Wonder* that Mort was looking for.

Without a pause Mort immediately snapped back, "Those by Stanley G. Weinbaum!"

Campbell studied Weinbaum's stories, digested them, stylized his scripts after them, and—BINGO!—a cent-a-word on acceptance check was soon on its way from *Standard*.

Campbell followed it up with a whole series of similar stories and sure sales.

When the first issue featuring one of his stories hit the stands, Campbell once again visited Mort for a planned interrogation.

"What did you do to my story?" a red-faced Campbell asked.

"I edited it," Mort replied. "That's what I get paid for!"

Campbell persisted. "Does that mean you get to change my story title to 'The Brain Stealers of Mars'?"

Mort quickly cut in. "It's more of a reader grabber than *your* quiet title!"

"And your readers want to read something called 'The Brain Stealers of Mars'?"

"Of course," Mort replied.

"Well, that's news to me," Campbell retorted. "All of my previous story titles appeared as I wrote them!" He thought for a moment, then added, "While I'm here let me ask you a few more questions. Why did you change so much of my copy?"

Mort answered, "Now, I told you that I didn't want a story that was so heavily laden down with so many science facts. Just get to Mars, and let the action begin! Just the adventure, period. I—that is, the reader—don't care how much or how little oxygen there is, how much water, or what the gravity is like. Just get the girl and get going!"

"Really? You can make changes in the story."

"Of course," Mort replied. "Leo Marguiles, our editorial director, is always looking over our shoulders to make sure that we are earning our keep with plenty of rewriting."

"Now, about the story's illustration," Campbell inquired further, "who chooses the scene?"

"Usually I hand the script to the artist and let him pick out an exciting one. But sometimes we are so close to deadline, I pick the scene and write up a short description for the artist."

"And after all the editing, that's it, right?"

"No, no," Mort corrected. "Then it goes to the printer, who sets it up on the linotype, and then it comes back here, and we have to proofread it."

"Er . . . proofreading? What's that?"

So Mort filled Campbell in about how proofreading is done and all about printer's marks and continued to answer all of the writer's questions on the publishing process.

Campbell finally got to the point where he said, "Just one more question. How do you always get the magazine to fit into your allotted pages?"

"Easy," Mort replied. "You just set all your stories, add in your advertising, and whatever pages are left blank you fill with letters to the editor."

Campbell stood up, thankfully shook Mort's hand, and said, "This has been a most instructive afternoon. I want you to be the first to know that before I came up here, I was informed that I was going to be hired as the new editor of *Astounding Stories* and I hardly had any idea of what an editor really does. Now thanks to you, I know."

(Though I had always held editors in awe, I sometimes forgot to remind myself that Mort more than occasionally chose to stretch the truth. Heck! One might say he used it as if it were a rubber band. So, many years later I was not really that surprised when Fred Pohl informed me that Mort's story of his "instruction of Campbell" was pretty much an out-and-out lie.

Actually it was editorial director Leo Marguiles who filled Campbell in about the dos and don'ts of editorial know-how when he landed the job.

Evidently, Mort's Campbell story was yet another Mortimer Weisinger lie, and given the reverence with which I held editors at the time, I felt badly misled.

Indeed, on one occasion Mort upset me with such an outrageous lie, a real whopper, that I told him I was going to have engraved on his tombstone, HERE LIES MORT WEISINGER—AS USUAL!)

Ed Hamilton (whom I now represented) and I became fast friends.

One particular time I was with him in California while he was working on the "Captain Future" stories, which appeared in the pulp magazine of the same title. Ed would usually write during the afternoons, and I would nap on a nearby couch. Back in those days, way before word processors, typewriters used to make a *ping* (like a small bell) whenever the typist came to the end of a line and had to move the carriage back to start a new line. I was familiar enough with Ed's scripts to know that he was averaging roughly ten words a line and that, since Hamilton was being paid the princely sum of a penny a word, the sound of each *ping* meant another penny for me since I was collecting a ten-percent commission.

Each *ping* was followed by my exultation: "Another penny!"

(This incident earned me a certain amount of fame and notoriety within the professional science fiction community of writers and editors and eventually found its way into a science-fiction detective novel entitled *Rocket to the Morgue* by Anthony Boucher.)

In my entire career as a literary agent, one of the high points of my years at Solar Sales Service was the sale of "The Accursed Galaxy" by Edmond Hamilton. It dealt with the theory that every galaxy is receding from our Earth's galaxy. I was so impressed with the story that I was determined to sell it to *Astounding*, a magazine market that the prolific Hamilton had never been able to crack. At that time it paid the highest rates in the field (Ed had been receiving a half cent per word from *Amazing* and *Wonder*, payable on publication). *Astounding* did exactly what I had hoped and bought it for a penny a word, payable on acceptance.

It worked!

It was a proud day for the Hamilton-Schwartz duo!

• • •

Years later I came up with a little ditty to describe my days as an agent, saying that the Solar Sales Service represented "Bradbury, Bester, Binder, Bracket, and Bloch, and that was just the Bs—and for the L of it, I also represented H. P. Lovecraft."

Now, Lovecraft was one of the star writers for *Weird Tales*, and through my contacts, I knew him to be very shy and reserved—but I knew I could get him a really good deal if I was just given the chance.

The two of us met at some literary gathering hosted by Donald Wandrei in 1935, and I asked him if he had any stories lying around that he had not yet been able to sell. With a forlorn look in his eye, he replied yes, that one of his tales—his longest to date at thirty-five thousand words—was still unsold, and he was depressed about it.

Frank Belknap Long and H. P. Lovecraft playfully trading blows.

He sent it to me. It was entitled "At the Mountains of Madness," and in a flash I sold it to F. Orlin Tremaine at *Astounding* for $350.

That check was the largest Lovecraft had ever received for a story.

Money was always tight for my dear Lovecraft (as I referred to him in our correspondence), and he would use penny postcards to save on expenses. He used to fill them with tiny script so that he could fit everything in. You almost needed a magnifying glass to read them.

With Mort off to greener pastures as an editor, Solar Sales Service was now completely my baby, and clients came from all different ways and means.

Henry Kuttner used to be a reader for Laurence D'Orsay, a California-based agent who ran ads in writers' magazines for would-be scribblers, offering to consider their materials for representation for a modest reading fee. Kuttner would read over a submission and decide whether or not it was worth D'Orsay's time to take the author on as a client in exchange for a share of the reading fee.

When Hank came across a science-fiction piece by a new writer by the name of Leigh Brackett, he decided that "this guy" had real potential and deserved better representation than D'Orsay would provide. Brackett deserved an agent who would work with "him" and find the right markets for the stuff "he" was turning out.

Indeed, figured Kuttner, Leigh Brackett deserved the same agent as his own. Brackett deserved the best! Brackett deserved Julius Schwartz, and who was I to disagree? So I took Leigh on as a client.

Needless to say, both Kuttner and I were pleasantly surprised to find out that Leigh the "he" was really a she!

LEIGH BRACKETT

I was soon placing Leigh's stuff—science fiction as well as mystery stories—with the pulps, and she became quite the successful writer in several genres.

I was fascinated by a real-life story she once told me. After she had sold a mystery novel, she was contacted by Howard Hawks to see if she might be willing to meet with him about a possible assignment. At the time she was working on a long novelette called Lorelei of the Red Mist, but not wanting to miss such a golden opportunity, she agreed and went to Hollywood to meet with Hawks—after persuading a young writer with whom she hung out at Muscle Beach by the name of Ray Bradbury to finish the yarn, which was eventually published in Planet Stories (Summer 1946 issue).

Needless to say, Hawks was quite surprised to see that Leigh was not a he, but since he liked her novel's tough-guy dialogue, he decided to give her a chance.

As it happens he was in a bind. He had signed up a certain literary light, as was the fashion in Hollywood at that time, and the celebrity author's drinking problem was delaying the completion of the screenplay, thus causing things to fall really behind schedule. As a result he needed another writer to come in and rescue the screenplay so that they could get on with the picture.

The celebrity writer in question was William Faulkner, and the picture was <u>The Big Sleep</u>. Leigh acquitted herself magnificently and thus set herself up nicely as a successful Hollywood screenwriter who worked with Hawks on numerous other films, including such John Wayne westerns as <u>Rio Lobo</u>. (Ironically her last screenwriting job was on her first science-fiction screenplay for the big screen—she was co-writer on a blockbuster picture of the 1980s called <u>The Empire Strikes Back</u>. As luck would have it, Leigh and I were scheduled to have lunch one day during my tenure at DC, and she arrived in a highly emotional state. She had just received word from her agent that George Lucas had chosen her to do the screenplay for the eagerly anticipated sequel to the science-fiction blockbuster <u>Star Wars</u>. It was tragic that she died before the most successful film that she ever worked on was released.)

While on a Hollywood assignment, Leigh used to rent a place at the Lawrence Welk Apartments. I remember that on a trip out to California, Leigh offered to secure me the use of a place there for the duration of my stay. I quickly accepted. I recall that she made me a delicious dinner of roast leg of lamb and oven-roasted potatoes. The memory of it still makes my mouth water.

Leigh married my good friend and client Ed Hamilton in a ceremony in California, with Ray Bradbury as best man.

By this time my client list included—in addition to Hamilton, Weinbaum, Lovecraft, Brackett, and Kuttner—such other notables as Manly Wade Wellman, John Taine, Ralph Milne Farley, J. Harvey Haggard, P. Schuyler Miller, Raymond Z. Gallun, Harl Vincent, Otto Binder, and from England, John Russel Fearn and Eric Frank Russell. (Soon I would even make a one-story sale for a former naval officer turned science-fiction writer by the name of Robert A. Heinlein.)

I didn't *really* have what anyone would call an office and pretty much worked out of my apartment or whatever phone booth I could find and fill with nickels.

On Thursday afternoons some of my clients and I would meet for lunch at Steuben's Tavern on Forty-seventh Street between Sixth Avenue and Broadway. Most of us would order the same thing: corned beef on rye, fries, and a beer (the only exception being Manly Wade Wellman who insisted on Dubonnet wine instead of beer)—all for about fifty cents.

Not all of my clients lived in the New York area, but whenever they (or other friends in the field) were in town, they would always join our Steuben gang for lunch. Some of the drop-ins included Frank Belknap Long, Otis Adelbert Kline, Jack Williamson, Horace Gold, David Vern (David V. Reed), L. Sprague de Camp, and Robert A. Heinlein.

Robert Bloch was a member of the Milwaukee Fictioneers, and when I showed up at one of their meetings in 1938, I cornered Bob and sweet-talked him into my being his agent. Bob was only twenty-one at the time and had been selling stories on his own to *Weird Tales* since right after his high school graduation. He decided that having an agent would be a good thing, and I was as good a choice as any. (Being from Wisconsin, he was no doubt unaware of my glorious reputation at the time.)

Bob handed me a couple of his *Weird Tales's* rejects, and on October 4 (less than two months later) I sold both of them to *Strange Stories* (they paid on acceptance whereas *Weird Tales* paid on publication). Both stories saw print in the February 1939 issue, with one published under the pen name Tarleton Fiske to avoid a double-Bloch byline in the table of contents.

Bob came East not long thereafter, claiming he wanted to see the 1939 New York World's Fair (he didn't realize that it wasn't located in Manhattan but rather in the borough of Queens). Bob plopped a nickel in the subway turnstile . . . and then vaulted over, (not realizing how it really worked, coming from a nonsubway metropolis like Milwaukee). When we finally got off the train at the fair's station, we stood on the elevated platform as Bob gazed at the futuristic never-never land skyline that was dominated by the Trylon and Perisphere, the symbol of the future. After a couple of minutes of awe-inspiring contemplation, he turned to me and said, "OK, I've seen enough of the World's Fair. Let's go back to Manhattan."

So we turned around, got on the train going in the opposite direction, and went back to the city, having never actually set foot on the fairgrounds.

(Though Bob's reactions to both the subway turnstiles

Schwartz and Bloch, together again in the 1980s. (Beth Gwinn)

and the World's Fair might seem a bit—how shall I say, eccentric—it was far from unique. On a subsequent trip to the fairgrounds, I witnessed the exact same behavior— jumping the turnstile and observing the fair's landscape without ever venturing onto the fairgrounds itself—from another visitor from even farther west, Jack Williamson!)

All told, I sold seventy-five Bob Bloch stories to a dozen different markets before I abandoned Solar Sales Services for an editorial position at DC Comics. My proudest sale for him was "Yours Truly, Jack the Ripper," which premiered in the July 1943 issue of *Weird Tales*. It was an eight-thousand-word story, and I negotiated eighty dollars for it (on publication, unfortunately, not even I could get *Weird Tales* to negotiate their boilerplate deal).

Forty-five years later, because of the Jack the Ripper connection, I secured him the assignment to write an introduction to "Gotham by Gaslight," a Batman Elseworlds story that involved speculation about the Ripper. Bob was paid five hundred dollars (on acceptance) for the assignment, which came out to about a dollar and a quarter a word. His rate sure had skyrocketed over the intervening years.

Even though I was their agent, I was still intimidated and awed by some of the writers (most of whom had a few years on me in terms of worldliness and maturity if not always actual age). Case in point, I remember being impressed by L. Sprague de Camp, a nonclient. He invited me out to a fancy restaurant, and I was completely awed by his *joie de vivre*, his *savoir faire*, the *je ne sais quoi*, and all that other French stuff. He wore his charm as easily as other men wore their hair.

I wanted to be a suave sophisticate just like him.

It had to be something corporeal or maybe something you could bottle and keep in a nifty silver case in your lapel like Maurice Chevalier did.

I did the easiest thing I could to emulate him. So when he took out a pack of Chesterfield cigarettes and offered me one, I took the bait—my first—and became hooked for thirty years before I woke up and quit.

(Years later in a de Camp tribute piece for *Lan's Lantern*, a Hugo award–winning fanzine, I wrote a piece that began:

L. Sprague de Camp, you could have been the death of me! It was just that those damn Chesterfields looked so good on you.

After meeting Manly Wade Wellman—the Dubonnet-drinking member of the Steuben gang—he once challenged me to sell one of his stories to a better market than he had been able to sell on his own. If I did, he would let me be his agent. So he gave me the story named "Space Station Number One," and I managed to sell it to *Argosy* (who called their SF "Different Stories" and paid more) at one and a quarter cents a word on acceptance. The story appeared in the October 10, 1936, issue, and as a result I had a new client and a lifelong friend.

Soon thereafter, Manly handed me a novella he had written entitled *Twice In Time*. He considered it to be the best thing that he had ever written, and he requested that I submit it to John W. Campbell at *Astounding* because he knew it would be right up Campbell's alley. He couldn't see how Campbell could possibly reject it. And so I did and gave it the extra-special hard sell, saying how wonderful Manly was, and left it for his review.

When I next showed up at Campbell's office, I asked him how he liked Manly's story. He said it was a sale—but only if Manly made a few changes. Campbell admitted that it was a great story but insisted that he wanted the ending rewritten.

I was crestfallen! I knew Manly wouldn't go for that. You couldn't rewrite the ending—it was the whole point of the story (the story dealt with a twentieth-century time traveler who goes back in time and introduces modern technology to the past. The last line is the hook: "My name is Leonardo da Vinci.")

I brought Campbell's response back to Manly, and he was

enraged, make that livid! Of course he would not change the story's surprise ending, and he vowed that he would get even with Campbell. And indeed he did eventually gain a sweet revenge on the editor who deigned to dishonor his work.

How? Here's how . . .

Manly then wrote a story that he knew Campbell couldn't turn down. It was entitled "Forces Must Balance," and it was just what Campbell would want. I sold it to him for *Astounding*. It featured a black-hearted villain named Mister Von Ghul. And unbeknownst to Campbell, "Von Ghu"— according to Wellman, who pronounced it *fongoo*—meant in Italian "fuck you," which was Manly's way of expressing his true feelings to Campbell for the way the editor had treated his masterpiece "Twice in Time." (The story eventually appeared in *Startling Stories* and even later in book form.)

TWO WRITERS BEGIN THEIR CAREERS

After Mort Weisinger became the editor of Thrilling Wonder Stories at Standard Magazines, he came up with a promotional stunt. He decided to hold a contest for new writers, with the winning entry to be published and earning an award of fifty dollars. At lunch one day Mort told me that the prizewinning story was "The Broken Axiom" by an unknown by the name of Alfred Bester. Mort didn't know him personally but was sure that "he's going to make it big in the pulps someday" and he wanted me to represent him and introduce him to the gang at Steuben's.

Years later Mort told me that he had only pretended

that Alfie's story was a contest entry (HERE LIES MORTIMER WEISINGER YET AGAIN . . . AND HE ADMITS IT!). The story had appeared unsolicited on his desk one day, and, liking it so much, it gave him the idea for boosting the magazine's circulation, while also calling attention to a really outstanding story by an unknown. He set the story aside for a while, announced the contest, and then pretended to rediscover the story as a contest entry and announce it as the winner.

Now, another new, previously unpublished writer was contemplating entering the contest and had indeed worked up a story for it. But he decided to pass because his story was pretty long (about seven thousand words), and, having a pretty good head for figures, he realized that he might make as much as twenty-five dollars more than the fifty-dollar prize if Campbell at <u>Astounding</u> picked it up instead.

His gamble paid off. Campbell read the story and bought it.

The story was "Lifeline," and the author was Robert A. Heinlein.

One wonders how history might have been different had Heinlein not looked at all of his options and decided to send the story to the contest at <u>Thrilling Wonder</u>. Since Bester's story already had "the fix" on winning, the story probably would have been automatically rejected. Perhaps Heinlein might have felt so dejected, he might have given up writing all together.

I guess we'll never know.

Back to Bester.

So I met Alfie; he got his fifty-dollar prize and the start of his literary career. Since Mort introduced him to me as "a promising and 'prize-winning' science-fiction author," naturally I expected him to write more science-fiction stories. As things would have it, though, his first two sales for me were in another genre (and, moreover, both sales occurred on the same day!).

It was June 28, 1940, and editor Ray Palmer of Ziff-Davis's *South Seas Stories* (who also edited *Amazing*) bought "Treasure on Camoia" for $135 and "The Man Who Was Tabu" for $60, both stories to be published in the October 1940 issue, with the latter story done under the house name of "Alexander Blade."

The first Bester science-fiction story I sold for him was "Life for Sale" to *Amazing*, a little over a month later, for $120, while the first story he submitted to me, "The Pet Nebula" I wound up having to bounce from one market to another. It was not sold until later and then only to *Astonishing Stories*, a secondary market at a half cent a word for the less than princely sum of $17.50.

One of the things I always remember about Alfie was that he always downplayed his talents as if he didn't really believe in them. Thirty years later, Alfie told me that one of the turning points in his life was April 2, 1942, when I sold his "The Dead Only Die Once" to *Unknown Worlds* for $350 (John W. Campbell, the editor, changed the title to "Hell is Forever" and published it in the August 1942 issue). According to Alfie, "Selling to *Unknown Worlds* was an electrifying experience" and the single most "big, big step up" in his confidence.

He figured that if he could make a sale to *Unknown Worlds* and John W. Campbell, then maybe he was a real writer after all. It was only then that he realized something that Mort and I had both recognized much earlier on.

Now, things were vastly different for science-fiction writers then.

Back in the 1930s—the so-called Golden Age of science fiction—there were no conventions (or other get-togethers) where writers could mingle, meet, and greet their fans. That is, until the first Science Fiction WorldCon in 1939.

Prior to that, members of the Queens Science Fiction League would occasionally get together. When I mentioned that I would be bringing along the professional science-fiction writer Ed Hamilton to the next meeting, the amount of people who wanted to attend doubled. Wow! An actual chance to meet a real live author!

On another occasion I brought along Otto Binder and Jack Williamson. Yet another sensational draw was Eric Frank Russell from Liverpool, who was in town on business thanks to my having sold his story "Sinister Barrier" to *Unknown Worlds* for $700.

It was literally a fan-meets-pro explosion!

When we saw what a draw these authors were, we immediately knew that they would be the key to the success of a convention.

When a little while later the notion of an Eastern Science

The Queens Science Fiction League, featuring a very young Isaac Asimov (second from right), circa 1938.

Fiction Convention was considered, I offered to bring in such professional writers as John W. Campbell. Eventually it was announced that a list of professionals in attendance would include L. Sprague de Camp, Frank Belknap Long, Otto and Jack Binder, and Otis Adelbert Kline. That convention, held in Newark on May 29, was a huge success, and it paved the way for the first WorldCon to be held on the following year in New York City.

That convention, NYCon I—the 1939 World Science Fiction Convention—was held in New York City on the July Fourth weekend in Caravan Hall on the second floor of a building off Fifth Avenue, opposite the Plaza Hotel. Originally we had hoped to have our convention in conjunction with and on site of the World's Fair that was being held in Flushing Meadows, not too far from where the Queens group used to meet. The fair's management was agreeable to having us as part of the overall event, but eventually we decided to back out when it became evident that all of our conventioneers would have to pay full fair admission—seventy-five cents—for each day of the convention, which would obviously be out of the question for the fans we hoped to bring in.

On opening day, convention chairman Sam Moskowitz blocked the door to make sure that no Commies or "Reds" could get in and disrupt our convention. He was the perfect guy to do the job because of his broad frame. He literally filled the doorway. You might say that was built like a truck driver (as a matter of fact he *was* a truck driver).

In addition to spreading the word among the pros to attend, I was delegated to coordinate the putting together of a souvenir program book printed for the convention. When Connie Ruppert offered to print it for sixty dollars (the way he did his fanzine), I solicited one-dollar sponsorships from fans who would be attending, and in turn they would have their names included in the book itself (I remember that a few pros like A. Merritt gave $10 to the cause, and I believe that both Ralph Milne Farley and Ray Palmer bought $10 ads. Some of the pages featured photos of several of the authors in attendance, as well.

The convention featured, in addition to the program book, a few other famous convention firsts. Forry Ackerman showed up in his "Things to Come"/Buck Rogers getup (thus inaugurating costumes at conventions), and I remember fans stopping Jack Williamson and L. Sprague de Camp on the street for their autographs (thus inaugurating convention signings). There was a guest of honor—the artist Frank R. Paul—and even a banquet that thirty-two people attended, a sumptuous feast of lamb chops, peas, and

French fries, with all of the trimmings including sherbet for dessert and all for a dollar, at the ultra swanky Wyndham Restaurant. (Ray Bradbury had to sit off to the side because he couldn't afford the meal at that time in his career since he had already borrowed money from Forry so that he could make the cross-country trek to the con.)

All in all, the con had two hundred people—a record that would stand until after World War II—which was not bad for something that had never really been done before.

L. Sprague de Camp signs for a fan at the first WorldCon author autographing.

WorldCon firsts: Forry Ackerman sports the first WorldCon "hall costume."

The first WorldCon "Dead Dog Party."

On the last day of the convention, Mort, Otto Binder, and I opted to play hooky and went to a ballgame instead. It was July Fourth, and the Yankees were playing a doubleheader that day. It was also Lou Gehrig Appreciation Day—the day he made his tearful farewell speech where he proudly proclaimed himself to be the luckiest man in the world.

I may have been a member of the first science fiction convention committee, but I was also a Yankees fan—and some things take precedence.

Another of the writers I repped was a guy by the name of Malcolm Jameson. Malcolm had served as an officer in the navy, and most of his stories treated spaceships as if they were submarines in outer space so that he could draw on his experience. (Note: Another submariner of the same era was the flaming red-haired young author L. Ron Hubbard, who dated Malcolm's daughter Vida. Vida was lusted after by many in our circle, but when she showed up on the arm of the flame-haired Romeo, we pretty much knew that we didn't have a chance. He was much too successful and too good-looking. Their affair didn't last too long, but the two of them as a couple were immortalized by Hannes Bok for a *Weird Tales* cover from 1939 that featured a robot menacing a man, obviously Ron, and a girl, even more obviously Vida.)

One meeting of our Steuben gang chanced to have Robert Heinlein and Malcolm in attendance, and I was eager to introduce them since they were both old navy men and therefore—so I thought—must have a lot in common.

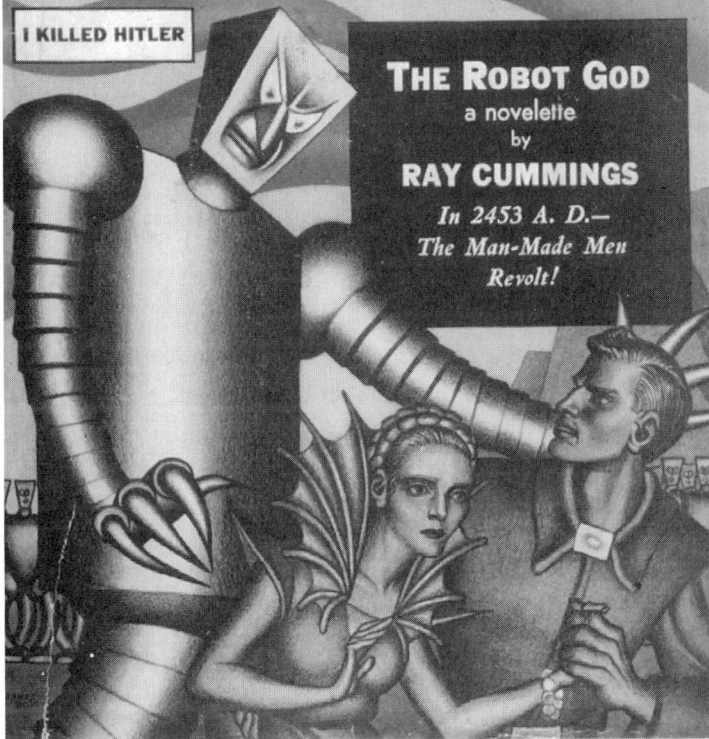

"The Case of Charles Dexter Ward"—LOVECRAFT
NOVEL

SEABURY QUINN,
CLARK ASHTON SMITH

JULY

Weird Tales

15¢

I KILLED HITLER

THE ROBOT GOD
a novelette
by
RAY CUMMINGS

In 2453 A. D.—
The Man-Made Men
Revolt!

A Weird Tales *cover featuring L. Ron Hubbard and Vida*
Jameson.

Heinlein was already a major author in great demand and Malcolm was eager to meet him.

As I introduced the two writers outside of our Steuben's lunching spot, commenting on their common background, Malcolm extended his hand to Heinlein. Heinlein responded with a curt and quick half of a handshake, where he barely touched Malcolm, and quickly drew his own hand back and continued on his way inside.

I was shocked, and dismayed! What was that all about? I had never seen Robert so brusque before.

Malcolm, on the other hand, had an explanation: "Heinlein was a grad of Annapolis, where I had only come up through the ranks in the navy. Officers of his rank and background don't usually fraternize with the rest of us."

Talk about class differences!

In some cases, I, too, fraternized among the ranks, occasionally mixing business with pleasure. On one occasion I was invited to spend a weekend with Henry Kuttner at the home he shared with his wife, Catherine L. Moore, at Hastings-on-Hudson in New York State (Kuttner sometimes wrote under the name Hastings Hudson).

About midnight, Catherine went upstairs to bed while Kuttner and I talked a while longer. When it was time for me to hit the sack on the spare cot downstairs in the area of the house where the two did their writing, Kuttner took his place on the other side of the room and set out to get some writing done. I eventually nodded off to the music of Henry Kuttner at the typewriter.

Kuttner quit work at about 4:00 A.M. and the sudden

interruption of keystrokes and his footsteps on the stairs woke me up. I turned over and was just nodding off again when the typewriter music began again with a slightly different pace and keystroke. Catherine had taken her husband's place and was picking up right where he left off.

They were really good collaborators, and their work together was sometimes so seamless that not even they could tell where one had left off and the other had started. Kuttner was a better plotter, but Catherine was the better craftsman in terms of literary ability.

Kuttner sometimes visited New York City on his own. On one such occasion in 1938 I took him out to Coney Island in Brooklyn, where a major landmark is a roller coaster called the Cyclone.

Kuttner took a good look at it and after a wild ride said, "I've got a great title for a story: "Lust Rides the Roller Coaster."

"What's it about?" I asked.

"I don't know," he replied, making a quick note of the title as we continued on our way.

I finally saw mention of the story in a book on the pulps by Frank Robinson. It was 1998, fifty years later, and there it was: a picture of a long-forgotten pulp magazine with a cover that screamed the title of the issue's lead story, "Lust Rides the Roller Coaster."

Kuttner wrote a story once about a fellow who meets a Martian in a bar. I was very taken with that story for some reason that I can't quite recall. When I heard in the early fifties that he had died suddenly, I started to have recurring dreams about him still being alive. In the dream I'd meet him at a bar (or walking down the street), and I call out "Henry!" But he'd never acknowledge me or admit that he was Kuttner because he was still afraid of the Martian from that story.

Before we knew it, WorldCon had become a fixed part of the yearly science-fiction community calendar, even if its location did move around from year to year.

The 1941 World Science Fiction Convention was in Denver, and Ed Hamilton and I decided to drive out there, then continue on to Los Angeles and hang out with the science fictioneers of the West Coast, many of whom we had only corresponded with.

In Denver, where Bob Heinlein was the convention's guest of honor, he had invited Hamilton and myself to visit him at his mountaintop home in Los Angeles, California, and we managed to see him two or three times a week during the month or so we spent on the West Coast.

"Listen, I really like you and Ed, and I like having you guys up at the house," Bob said on our third or fourth visit. "But I've got a problem with that noisy kid you always bring along. He's a loudmouth, asks too many questions, and he always upsets everything. No more, please. Just leave him home next time, please?"

That young kid was the first client I took on who was not already an established writer—a "pro"—at the time I agreed to represent him. He was a twenty-one-year-old paperboy, and while I was in Los Angeles I had taken the opportunity to hand deliver him a check for his first accepted story. From that moment on Ed and I couldn't seem to get rid of him.

I had met him previously at the 1939 New York Science Fiction Convention (where I also finally got to meet F. R. Paul, the "Paul" whose artwork caught my eye on my issue of *Amazing*). The lad had also attended the convention determined to (1) attend the con and also see the World's Fair, (2) sell the artwork of Hannes Bok to *Weird Tales*'s editor, Farnsworth Wright, and (3) convince a big-time New York literary agent—*moi*—to become his agent. To fulfill his threefold ambitions, he borrowed fifty or so dollars from Forrest J Ackerman for travel expenses.

The persistent kid wouldn't take no for an answer, and so the young new writer by the name of Ray Bradbury talked

Forry Ackerman agrees to loan Ray Bradbury the money to attend WorldCon.

me into taking him on as a client. I ended up telling him to send me his short stories, and I would get back to him.

So he did (sometimes sporadically because he had to wait until he had enough to cover the cross-country postage), and invariably I would bat them back to him with criticism, usually about their content. But not too long after, I started to notice that he was a pretty good writer. He was barely out of his teens, and he was already writing prose that rivaled my seasoned professional clients of the Steuben gang.

Finally in 1941 I made a sale for him to *Super Science Stories*, a fifty-five-hundred-word story called the "The Pendulum," which he had written with an assist by Henry Hasse, at a half-cent a word. I had been planning the California trip with Hamilton when I got the good word on the sale, and rather than mail the check (for the princely sum of $27.50 less my commission), I had decided to bring it with me and deliver it in person so that I could see the look on his face.

Leaving New York by train, I met Hamilton down in Pittsburgh, and we drove west by day and well into the night. Hamilton planned on selling his car in Los Angeles because at that time, due to the state's sparse population, you could get more money for a used car there than back East.

We journeyed west with a side trip along the way to see Edwin K. "Ted" Sloat, a science-fiction writer living in Iowa (at the time I was twenty-six and Ed was in his middle thirties, two freewheeling guys looking for a good time). Ted took us to the local Elk's club and bought us a few rounds of drinks, and for the first time in my life I got loaded. Hamilton and I were so bombed that when we finally staggered back to our motel, neither of us could maneuver the key into the lock of our door (not even the magic words "Open Sesame!" worked), and we had to summon a clerk for assistance. Hamilton never let me live this incident down, and I can still hear him saying over and over again, "Wellman would be proud of you!"

The two of us wandered around Los Angeles a bit before we arranged to a stay at a little rental cottage on Norton off Olympic Boulevard.

Famished after our long trip and the toil of unpacking, we hiked down the street to find a place to eat and maybe a newspaper. And there on the corner of Olympic, hawking newspapers, was a young "polar bearish looking" kid by the name of Ray Bradbury, whose inaugural story I had recently sold.

I'll never forget the happy, happy look on his face when I told him that he had sold his first story.

Ray was on his way!

The story appeared in the November 1941 *Super Science Stories* which appeared on the newsstand on August 22— the very day of Ray's 21st birthday!

THE MAÑANA LITERARY SOCIETY

Los Angeles was home in those days to a loose-knit group of writers who called themselves the Mañana Literary Society. Mañana (Spanish for "tomorrow") because even in the days when Los Angeles was a small town, the Southern California laid-back character had

begun to take hold: They'd get the manuscript done
<u>tomorrow</u>.

They met and hung out at the top of Lookout Mountain
in the home of Robert A. Heinlein, who never served booze
to his guests. "If I did," Heinlein said, pointing out the
hairpin turns and steep drop-offs along the road to his
house, "I could wipe out my competition overnight."

Among Mañana's members was Erma Mintz. Heinlein took
one of her rejected manuscripts, rewrote, and then sent it
on to John Campbell. When Campbell rejected it, Robert gave
it to me to try and sell. I sent it around and eventually sold
it to <u>Astonishing Stories</u> for $21.50, and it was published in
the April 1941 issue under the byline of Lyle Monroe.

Ray would come over in the afternoon after selling papers
and ask our opinions on story ideas and other projects he
was working on. Our place became the hangout that month
for the Los Angeles Science Fiction League, where we would
gossip and party and exchange ideas and swap stories.
Everyone drank beer (except Ray, who stuck to Coke).

Sometime in 1942, because of the dearth of markets for fantasy and science-fiction short stories, I persuaded Ray to
broaden his output and perhaps take a crack at a
detective/mystery story or two. Sure enough, he soon sent me
one with the title "The Long Night," but before I had the
chance to submit it anywhere, I got a telegram from Ray that
said, "Please insert the following paragraph onto the end of my
story. I forgot to include the motivation for the crime."

I submitted the story to my friend W. Ryerson Johnson at

"VIPs" of the Los Angeles Science Fiction Society (standing: Robert A. Heinlein, Jack Williamson, Forrest J Ackerman, Walter Daugherty, Charles Hornig; seated: Russ Hodgkiss, Arthur K. Barnes, Edward "Doc" Smith, Ed Hamilton, Franklyn Brady).

Popular Publications. Upon my next visit, he greeted me with a check for $87.50, raving about the story and assuring me that he would personally edit it himself, all along asking for more from this new talent by the name of Ray Bradbury.

Sometime later Ray served as Ed Hamilton's best man at his wedding to Leigh Brackett (later on he'd also serve as best man at the wedding of friend and cinematic special-effects pioneer Ray Harryhausen, with whom he had built model dinosaurs during his boyhood).

Leigh Brackett was one of his oldest friends, and he regarded her as sort of his literary mentor and teacher even before he had met Ed and me. He would hang out with her at Muscle Beach and kick around story ideas. Undoubtedly he picked up a thing or two from her, particularly in the area of mystery-fiction writing.

After selling Ray's first seventy stories, I told him I could no longer serve as his literary agent because I had been hired as a full-time editor at All American Comics.

Ed Hamilton always liked to make an annual trip to New York in the spring, usually around April, because as he was extremely fond of bock beer, which was at that time only available for a few weeks. (My goyim friend informs me that bock beer was produced for Lent; its added body and richness was used by the brewing monks of old to help them get through their Lenten fast.)

Even after I had left the science-fiction field for the then greener pastures of comics, the Hamilton's and I still tried to keep in close touch.

One time they came to New York, the Hamiltons and me and my wife, Jean, along with a young comic book artist by the name of Gil Kane (whose favorite all-time fantasy yarn was a piece from *Weird Tales* by Hamilton entitled "He Who Hath Wings"—needless to say Gil was a major fan) all ate at a place called the Blue Ribbon Café, a popular hangout for showbiz people. We were later joined by some friend of theirs. I also remember us catching a glimpse of an Broadway actor and soon to be movie star by the name of Walter Matthau.

A great time was had by all!

Another time on the way home from an around-the-world trip, Ed and Leigh came to New York and planned to spend a week so that they could spend more time with Jean and me. Unfortunately Jean and I had already made other plans. We, ironically, were flying out to California to visit our daughter and son-in-law (he was at the time on sabbatical out there) the next day, and as luck would have it we would not be able to stick around New York to spend time with them. We gave them the phone number where we could be reached on the West Coast and set out on our previously planned trip.

The evening of the day we arrived in California, lo and behold we received a phone call from our friends the Hamiltons. They had decided to cut short their say in New York and follow us out to the coast so that they would not miss the chance of spending time with us. They invited us over to their home for dinner a couple of days later.

Having just been pleasantly surprised ourselves, Jean and I decided to return the favor with a little pleasant surprise for the Hamiltons. We decided to call our mutual friend and Ed's best man, Ray Bradbury, to join us for the dinner that night.

Ray rendezvoused with us, and we all showed up at their door.

Leigh and Ed were surprised. They didn't just do a double take, they did a triple take. They were overjoyed!

Dinner was my favorite—a salmon loaf (at my special request) made deliciously by our hostess—and we had the time of our lives. Sadly there was not much time left for Ed—he died shortly after that. (Years later, Leigh told me that Ed had told her that in retrospect that night was indeed Ed's favorite night of his life).

PART THREE

MY ENTRANCE TO THE WONDERFUL WORLD OF COMICS

In the early 1940s, and partially thanks to Mort's and my initial efforts on his behalf, Alfred Bester became quite a successful science-fiction writer and was quite literally selling everything he wrote. But as a married man with a family and an expensive apartment on Manhattan's fashionable Sutton Place, he eventually had to find another means of supporting himself, partially due to the declining number of science-fiction magazines that were available to buy his stories (even a super-agent like Schwartz couldn't sell a story unless there was someone there to buy it and publish it).

Alfie became concerned and went to his discoverer, Mort Weisinger, to ask his advice.

Mort thought for a moment and suggested that Alfie consider taking a crack at the wide-open market of comics as a sideline.

Alfie considered the idea but admitted that he really didn't know anything about comics, nor could he recall ever having read any, and asked Mort if he would more or less break him in.

Mort did him one better: He introduced him to the best writer of comics he knew, a guy named Bill Finger, the writer-creator of probably the most famous nonsuper comic book hero, the world's greatest detective, Batman (as well as such other comic book heroes as the Green Lantern).

(Now, hold on! I know that everyone has heard that Bob Kane is the creator of Batman, and from the character's debut in *Detective Comics* #27 in June of 1939, the only name credited on all of the stories is Bob—originally Robert—Kane. The real story is that back in 1938, when *Superman* was a big hit, its editor—a fellow by the name of Vince Sullivan—wanted to try to duplicate its success with a similar sort of hero.

So Vince went to a young cartoonist named Bob Kane, who was only twenty-two at the time, and asked him to come up with a similar costumed character hero, and he would be willing to give it a try. He even suggested that for inspiration he might look to a movie that featured a story about a bat.

So off Bob went and came back with a sketch. Vince liked what he saw and told Bob to come back with the story. Now, Kane wasn't a storyteller. He was an illustrator, so he got his close friend Bill Finger—a rabid fan of the pulps, which featured numerous masked mystery heroes—to flesh out a story line and a background for his creation. Editor Sullivan liked the final product that was delivered to him, and the rest is Bat-history!

So the actual truth of the matter is, Bob Kane may have drawn Batman, but it was Bill Finger who came up with the back story, Wayne manor, Alfred the butler, and all of those memorable villains in the Batman universe such as the Joker and the Catwoman.)

So comics amateur Alfie sat down with comics professional Bill the veteran and learned all about good comic book writing . . . and, as expected, Alfie was a fast learner.

When he was ready, Mort gave him an assignment on a comic about a character named Genius Jones (loosely based on a character called "the Human Encyclopedia" that Mort ran when he was a pulp editor). Alfie, of course, did a fine job on it. Not too soon afterward, Mort called Alfie in for a new assignment. It turned out that All American Comics was in desperate need of a new writer for *Green Lantern* and Mort enthusiastically recommended Alfie for the job because he felt that Alfie wanted the steady work and would probably enjoy it more than the short one-shots that he had been assigning him.

So Alfie subwayed down to All American Comics and took over the *Green Lantern* stories.

Notice, if you will, the similarities between the following bits of poetry:

In brightest day, in blackest night,
No evil shall escape my sight!

Let those who worship evil's might
Beware my power—Green Lantern's light!

and

Gully Foyle is my name
And Terra is my nation.
Deep space is my dwelling place,
The stars my destination.

Both were written by Alfred Bester.

While I was still acting as his agent, Alfie and I had become close friends, and he frequently invited me home for dinner and to play cards (he was a terrible card player, but I didn't mind playing with him; his favorite game was Hearts). One momentous evening, Alfie told me that there was trouble down at All American Comics because the assistant editor was leaving, and the chief editor, Shelly Mayer—already too busy with other duties—needed an assistant to plot stories, edit scripts, and proofread pages.

Alfred Bester.

Alfie suggested—no, insisted—that I apply for the job. He knew that the very same narrowing of the market that had made things financially tight for him as a science-fiction writer was no doubt making things tight for me as a science-fiction agent.

Like Alfie in his conversation with Mort, I, too, had to admit that I really didn't know anything about comics, let alone about editing them.

Alfie said not to worry; he had already set up an interview for me on the following day, and all I really needed to do was to pick up two or three comics that I could read on the way in to acquaint myself with them and give me something to talk about during the interview.

So on my way to the subway station I went to the newsstand and picked up three All American Comics. They cost a dime apiece back then, and to this day that thirty cents was the only money that I have ever spent on comics in my entire career. But it turned out to be the best investment in my life because the interview went well, and I was hired on February 21, 1944. Like Mort Weisinger before me, another fannish kid from the Bronx was finally becoming an editor, just like the gray masters of whom I had been in awe of in my youth, the "gods on earth." (Note: I couldn't start work until February 23 because in those days February 22 was celebrated as a holiday for George Washington's birthday—as this was before we adopted the custom of having a moveable holiday that would make a three-day weekend called President's Day.)

Years later, leaping ahead to 1987, the Science Fiction Writers of America elected Alfie as Grand Master. That same year he was also slated to be the guest of honor at 1987 Science Fiction Worldcon in Brighton, England, but because of illness he was unable to attend in person. Instead, he asked if he could do his guest of honor speech on video, and they said fine and asked if he would consent to a follow-up video interview, as well, to which he agreed.

When the committee then asked him who he wanted to conduct the interview, he immediately snapped back (horror of horrors!) that he wanted Julie Schwartz to do it—in fact, he insisted on it!

Now, Alfred Bester had quite a reputation as editor of *Holiday* magazine and was an A-#1 celebrity interviewer in the U.S. who had interviewed such public figures as the Queen of England and Sophia Loren herself . . . and here I, a neophyte interviewer at best and at the time a nobody of note in science-fiction circles, was going to interview him, so I had to ask him, *Why me?*—a rank amateur!

Alfie thought about it for a second and bellowed over the phone, "For revenge!" He started to laugh . . . and I laughed back! He laughed louder and so did I. . . . And with a final laugh he hung up the phone.

Unfortunately Alfie passed away shortly after that, and I never got to do the interview. I also never found out what he meant by "for revenge," for that matter.

Shortly before he died, ailing Alfie was confined to a veteran's hospital, and I mentioned this to my good friend Harlan Ellison. Harlan had once told me that he would rather receive a compliment on his work by Alfred Bester than a million-dollar book contract. When Harlan learned

MAN OF TWO WORLDS

that Alfie was in the hospital and might be dying, he imme-diately phoned the hospital and told them that he was doing a story for a major media outlet on the very important and celebrated writer Alfred Bester, who was currently in their care and that he was going to require twice-daily reports on Alfie's health and well-being—thus encouraging them to give the best possible care.

Alas, Alfie died a day or so later.

When it came time for the Science Fiction Writers of America's annual Nebula Awards banquet (which was held that year in Los Angeles) where Alfie's Grand Master Award was being handed out, I had a friendly tussle with the then super literary agent Kirby McCauley (who in addition to representing Alfie also at the time represented such big shots as Stephen King and Robert Silverberg), who thought that he should accept the award for Alfie until I explained to him that I had been Alfie's first agent. So in perfect profes-sional courtesy I had priority!

Of course, I wasn't willing to lug the heavy thing back East, so Harlan offered to hold on to it for safekeeping.

Max Gaines, the publisher of All American Comics (and father of William Gaines, legendary founder of *MAD* maga-zine) came up with the idea of a *really big* comic book that would be called *The Big All-American Comic Book* and would feature stories of all of the heroes in the line—some fifteen of them in total. It would be a big, fat book (132 pages) for just twenty-five cents and for which I contributed a Johnny Thunder story. All the employees were contributors, and all the editors and heads of production would share in the royalties!

A couple of days after the book hit the newsstands, a smiling Max Gaines came around and said that it looked like it was going to be such a big success that rather than waiting the mandatory time it would take for royalty accounting, he had decided to share the wealth and give each of us a check for $250 (roughly four times my weekly salary) as a flat payment instead.

We were all thrilled at his generosity.

Only later did we find out how well the issue really sold and that we probably all would have made at least four times as much had we stuck to our original royalty agreements.

THE DRAFTING OF SCHWARTZ

With the storms of World War II approaching, I received my draft notice and was dismayed to see that I was unlucky enough to have had a very low number and would therefore be among the first drafted.

Sure enough, I got the call and was summoned down to the Draft Bureau—which at that time was located at 480 Lexington Avenue—where I was to be examined. When we got to the eye exam part, the doctor asked me to read the fourth line of the chart without my glasses, and I replied that I couldn't. The doctor then tested my glasses on a machine and ascertained that indeed my eyesight was just as bad as I claimed (and that I wasn't faking my extreme nearsightedness).

I was sent home and soon after received a card in the

mail notifying me that I had been classified as 4F and ineligible for service.

Lucky me!

Evidently as the war went on, the service lowered its eligibility standards because my wife had a cousin who had a higher number than I did who was later called up and accepted for service for clerical work—despite the fact that he had a glass eye. So my low number in the beginning turned out not to be bad luck but rather good luck.

During the war years I continued as an agent, until that memorable day that I went down at Alfie's urging to 80 Lafayette to apply for a job.

Within months after being hired, All American Comics combined with DC Comics, and we had to move uptown to their offices, which were now located at 480 Lexington Avenue—the same address as the Draft Bureau where I had reported a few years back.

Ironically, it turned out that I eventually was drafted by DC Comics instead of the army and wound up on a tour of duty that definitely outlasted the war.

The offices at 480 Lexington were set up along a long corridor right off the elevator. The first office was editorial director Whit Ellsworth; next the Mort Weisinger and Jack Schiff department; coeditors Robert Kanigher and I shared the end offices farther down the hall.

The other editorial offices were lined up along the wall, and on the opposite side was the production department, where they put the pages together and corrected the art-

Yours truly, hard at work in the 1950s.

work and touched up the lettering in preparation for the printer and the publication of the magazines.

My script-writing career consisted of a *Green Lantern* story (reprinted in issue #3 of *The Amazing World of DC Comics*), a western story for *Foley of the Fighting Fifth*, and the aforementioned *Johnny Thunder*, along with scores of filler page features such as "Strange Realm of the Atom!" and "Science Says You're Wrong If You Believe That . . ."

In deference to our friendship, Alfie Bester stayed with *Green Lantern* for a year after I came on board, before he moved on to radio scripts (for such programs as *The Shadow* and *Charlie Chan*), prose fiction, and *Holiday* magazine, thus leaving me with the unenviable task of finding a replacement for him. It quickly dawned on me that maybe I could replace him with another writer from my Solar Service client list. My first choice was Henry Kuttner.

I wound up, made my pitch, and quickly struck out. Horror of horrors, he turned me down emphatically.

So I stepped up to the plate to try again.

This time I went to bat, hit him with a copy of *Green Lantern* . . . he caught it . . . but I was still called out! (Out of luck, that is.) He wasn't interested. Sure he read it, even liked it, but he still didn't want to do it.

That was when fate intervened.

Somehow a copy fell into the hands of his lovely wife, Catherine Moore Kuttner. She read it and fell in love with one of the characters and insisted that Kuttner accept the assignment. And like any obedient husband he did.

(That character was a derbied cabbie by the name of Doiby Dickles whose motto was "Soivice wot don't make youse noivous." Whenever Doiby spotted a crime from his cab, he shot off a rocket into the night sky that burst into flames and alerted Green Lantern that a crime was in progress. I was often asked about just how often a cabbie was going to come across a crime in progress, and my standard answer was, probably more often than Batman and Robin would while looking down from some rooftop high above Gotham City streets at midnight.)

Within a year Kuttner left to follow in Alfred Bester's noncomic footsteps—but not before he had created a truly memorable villain with the lovable name of Valentine Sweetheart. I looked for another replacement and tried to convince Dave

Vern to come on board. Dave also gave me a resounding "NO" but instead recommended his friend John Broome, whom I now like to refer to as my best friend, one of my best writers, and indeed the best man at my wedding. John took over *Green Lantern*, and together with such artists as Paul Reinman, Irwin Hasen (the creator of the popular syndicated strip *Dondi*), and Alex Toth (later of *Space Ghost* fame) under my tutelage, we took the Golden Age *Green Lantern* to new heights of success, eventually revamping him completely as a new character drawn by Gil Kane and modeled loosely on his neighbor at one time, the popular actor Paul Newman.

On *Green Lantern* we moved his ring hand from the left to the right, changed his point of vulnerability, and eventually added an oversight committee of the cosmos called "the Guardians of the Universe." John and I didn't have much of

Gil Kane. (Beth Gwinn)

an idea about who the Guardians really were, and we basically took their name from an old Captain Comet story that John had previously scripted (*Strange Adventures* #22 "The Guardians of the Clockwork Universe"). Putting our heads together for an alien switch, we decided that all of the Guardians should look alike because basically in all comics *all* aliens look alike. Gil Kane then based their general appearance on the prime minister of Israel at the time, David Ben-Gurion.

We also gave the new Green Lantern a second identity in the far future of 5700 A.D. We chose that date at random by just looking at the telephone in my office: at the time DC's number was PLaza 9-5700.

One of the writers from my former agenting stable who indulged me with a story assignment in my new field was Robert Bloch. We didn't put author and artist credits on comic book stories in those days, but for Bob Bloch completists, he was the scripter of "The Flash and the Black Widow," in the August/September 1945 issue of *Flash Comics* #66. It was a hell of a good story, but when I tried to get him to write another, he simply grumbled "Once was enough," and I never brought it up again.

Otto Binder used to write stories with his brother Earl under the pen name of Eando Binder (E and O Binder) when I was their agent. When Otto gave up writing SF stories, he, too, took to writing comics, and eventually he wrote over five hundred stories featuring Captain Marvel.

Now, the corporation for whom I worked eventually came to the decision that Captain Marvel was way too close to Superman and sued the company, eventually putting them out of business and making them turn Captain Marvel over to DC. As a result, Otto also came on board and turned his talents to writing *Superman*.

By 1950 the Golden Age of comics faded away because superheroes were waning in their popularity (and newsstand sales). The only three biggies who survived this drop in popularity were Superman, Batman, and Wonder Woman. So to fill out the list, we launched a new line of comics based on westerns, science fiction, and characters adapted from radio and cartoons and the new kid on the block that was called television. There were comic book series based on Phil Silvers's popular *Sergeant Bilko* show, *Mr. District Attorney*, Jackie Gleason, Bob Hope, Charlie Chan, and *Gangbusters* as well as various cartoons such as *Fox and Crow*, the *Three Mouseketeers*, etc. Some would have a healthy run, but eventually sales would drop, and we would be looking for new titles to replace them with.

But my favorite of favorites were the science-fiction comics, *Strange Adventures* and *Mystery in Space*, and when I was assigned the editorship of these two titles, a lifelong dream was fulfilled.

Finally, I was a science-fiction editor, one of the gods on earth!

•　•　•

I remember when I got Virgil Finlay to work for me. He was one the top SF artists of his time.

He used to do sketches in this restaurant in the '40s that they would then hang on the wall, and he would eat there free for a week.

We met there once, and I told him I had a story that I needed done, and he wanted to do it, but I needed it too fast because Finlay always drew everything to exact size, and the art would then be stippled. I was hoping for just a cover, but he said he would do the whole thing and he did—and it still met our deadline. (He really needed the money!)

The story was "The Mad Planet" and it appeared in *Mystery in Space #19* (the script was by Sid Gerson).

"The Counterfeit Earth," another story, was based on a cover. It showed two Earths and a returning spaceman being told that if he landed on the real Earth, the planet would be spared . . . but if he landed on the counterfeit Earth, the world would be destroyed.

Now, Otto Binder was knowledgeable enough to know that from outer space, the only structure that you could really make out was the Great Wall of China, and he figured that into the story. It was illustrated by Joe Kubert and appeared in *Mystery in Space #35*.

Mystery in Space comics were the basis for a series of reprint comics that I edited later on called *From Beyond the Unknown.*

The title *Mystery in Space* came into being in an interesting way. *Strange Adventures* was doing very well, particularly with the gorilla covers. (For example, *Strange Adventures* had had a particularly successful issue that featured a gorilla in a cage holding up a sign that indicated that he was really a man who had been the victim of an experiment that had gone awry, thus starting a trend in cover art featuring gorillas—all of which, incidentally, sold better than those without gorillas on them.)

Following *Strange Adventures*'s success, Whit Ellsworth, who was editorial director, called me in and said that he wanted me to put out another science-fiction comic, and I said that it would be impossible because there were no titles left—at the time there were so many pulp magazines out there that all of the good titles had been already taken.

"No problem," he snapped back. "I already have the title: *Mystery in Space*."

"Oh," I replied, acknowledging that it was a good title and adding, "These will be mystery stories that take place in interplanetary settings—sort of adventure stories."

"No," he quickly corrected me, "just use the same type of stories you've been using in *Strange Adventures* and put them in *Mystery in Space*, too."

"Then why are we using that title?" I asked. "Space I can see because the stories take place there, and space means science fiction . . . but mystery?"

Whit explained. "We've also been putting out mystery magazines, and they are selling pretty well, so *Mystery in Space* is a good commercial title, a good selling title: It has a hook for both mystery readers and science-fiction readers."

Strange Adventures #8: *the issue that launched a thousand gorillas.* (©2000 DC Comics)

So who wanders into the office of couple of days later but a young fellow—an illustrator—looking for work. Editor Murray Boltinoff had nothing for him, so he told him to go see Julie, and this fellow by the name of Frank did.

I gave him a job to do for something called "Spores in Space" for the inaugural issue of *Mystery in Space* that had been written by Gardner Fox.

So what's the big deal? That young illustrator was Frank Frazetta!

We only worked together on that one title—"Spores in Space"—but we renewed acquaintances several years later at a Writers of the Future get-together when he was doing covers for them.

"Star Hawkins" was a takeoff on a Humphrey Bogart-type of detective who had an assistant, a Dr. Watson type, Ilda the robot. When we were doing the science-fiction series, I thought it would be a good idea to have a detective who had a robot as an assistant, and when money got tight, he would have to pawn her to get some cash to pay the rent and make ends meet until he could get the funds to get her back.

"Star Rovers," happened when I decided to do an adventure story with three adventureers in outer space who come upon a planet and explore it, and certain strange things would happen . . . and when they got together later on to discuss what happened, even though they all saw the same thing, each one had a different interpretation of what had happened. Three different stories based on the same events—sort of a *Rashomon* in outer space.

I used the writers' names on the story and on the cover initially, like Otto Binder and Edmond Hamilton and Henry Kuttner, in order to attract some of their readership from the pulp magazines . . . but I was quickly ordered to refrain from doing so by the top brass.

(I eventually had to give up *Strange Adventures* to do *Batman* at the instruction of my boss at the time, Irwin Donenfeld.)

THE ATOMIC KNIGHTS

"The Atomic Knights" was a post-World War III series that ran in <u>Strange Adventures</u> comic books that featured a group of postapocalypic knights (whose armored suits protected them from harmful residual radiation) riding mutated Dalmatians from city to city while going on quests to bring about justice. John Broome (writer) and Murphy Anderson (artist) were the regular team on this assignment.

One of the fun things about the Knights was that each story would take place in a different postholocaust city. We had "Danger in Detroit," "The Cavemen of New York," "The Lost City of Los Angeles," and—my favorite—the Dixieland-jazz inspired "The King of New Orleans" (now on display in the Mardi Gras Museum in New Orleans, Louisiana, as part of their exhibition of Mardi Gras memorabilia) which included the Knights taking part in a Mardi Gras jazz parade.

Ranking high among my science-fiction series in comics were the Adam Strange stories (all written by Gardner Fox), which made their debut in *Showcase*.

Gardner Fox was a graduate of St. John's Law School. Though he never actually practiced law, he always thought like a lawyer—he was organized, meticulous, and he never walked into his editor's office without knowing what he was going do. He plotted stories with me the exact same way, and he never sat down to write a story without knowing every twist and turn it would take. He was always fully prepared, the perfect Boy Scout.

Gardner came in one day, and we decided to do a new series that was more or less inspired by Burroughs's *John Carter of Mars*. Now, we had to figure out how to get him out to that star system, so we came up with the zeta beam. And the beauty of the science of an Adam Strange story was that he would have to get to the exact spot where the zeta beam would strike to get him there, so that would be part of the story. (I gave him his name: "Adam" because he was the first and "Strange" because he had "Strange Adventures.")

Now, science dictated that you could only see Alpha Centauri from below the equator, so we always had to get Adam down there to hook up with it. It couldn't be in Hollywood or New York. I remember we set one down in Rio during Carnival and another in the South Pacific.

Adam found a love interest on Rann by the name of Alanna . . . but was always teleported back to Earth at a critical, or at least inconvenient, moment.

We would come up with a premise and then do a story around it. And, incidentally, Sardath, the father of Alanna, was based on an Infantino characterization of *me* (JS).

SCIENCE-FICTION FILLERS

Though I never really fancied myself a comic writer, I did do the fillers in the science-fiction comics when the story would end midpage—titles like "Giants of the Telescope," "Strange Realm of the Atom," "It's Hard to Believe But . . . ," and "Science Says You're Wrong If You Believe That . . . ," which would illustrate some facet of science or debunk some popular misconception. I was paid eleven dollars a page for writing them (and also got the opportunity to show off some of what I'd picked up when I earned my degree in math and physics).

Mort Drucker, later of <u>MAD</u> magazine fame, broke into the business providing the illustrations for some of these fillers.

Showcase proved to be quite a useful title for us and provided the basis for many of my successful reworkings of characters.

Now, when you put out a magazine for a new title in, say, January, at the time it goes on sale, you already have the February issue done, the art completed for the March issue, and the script in the hopper for the April issue.

You were always four months ahead, and it usually took three to five months to get an indication of how a given issue's sales were because back then all of your distribution was through the newsstands. And that was in the days

SCIENCE says you're WRONG if you BELIEVE THAT

PLANETS AND STARS SHINE WITH THE SAME LIGHT...

AS THE PLANET VENUS REVOLVES AROUND THE SUN IT GOES THROUGH A SERIES OF PHASES EXACTLY AS DOES THE EARTH'S MOON!

STARS ARE LUMINOUS AND GIVE OFF THEIR OWN LIGHT. PLANETS REFLECT THE LIGHT THAT FALLS ON THEM FROM A STAR.

A PERSON'S HEIGHT REMAINS CONSTANT THROUGH 24 HOURS...

-6 FEET 1½ INCHES 7 A.M. -6 FEET 11 P.M.

A PERSON'S HEIGHT MAY VARY AS MUCH AS 1¼ INCHES, ESPECIALLY IN TALL YOUNG PEOPLE. ONE IS TALLEST IN THE MORNING, JUST AFTER RISING WHEN THE CARTILAGE SURFACES WHICH SEPARATE THE BONES OF THE SPINAL COLUMN ARE EXPANDED. DURING THE DAY, THE ERECT POSITION CAUSES THE CARTILAGE SURFACES TO BE SQUEEZED TOGETHER, RESTORING ONE'S TRUE HEIGHT.

FISH IS A BRAIN FOOD...

FISH CONTAIN NO FOOD ELEMENTS ESPECIALLY ADAPTED TO THE BUILDING OR RENOVATING OF THE BRAIN. NO ONE FOOD IS MORE BENEFICIAL TO THE BRAIN THAN ANY OTHER.

THERE ARE PLACES ON EARTH WHERE IT NEVER RAINS...'

ALL REGIONS OF THE WORLD HAVE OCCASIONAL RAINS. EVEN THE DESERTS GET AN INCH OR TWO OF RAIN DURING THE YEAR.

One of my scientific filler pages. (©2000 DC Comics)

before computer tracking, when covers of the comics could eventually be returned for credit—thus making the final sales reckoning of a given title a slow process indeed.

Now, if the first issue didn't do well, you usually wound up with diminishing sales on the second, third, etc., all of which were too far along to cancel. Our idea on *Showcase* was simple. We would use it to put out a single issue showcasing a new character or concept, then wait to see how it sold before we turned it into a regular monthly title. *Showcase* could function as a sort of one-shot comic trial balloon.

The first three *Showcases* flopped, and we were at an editorial meeting trying to decide what to do in number four when I suggested that we try to revive the Flash, who had died with the demise of the other superhero titles (with the exception of Superman, Batman, and Wonder Woman).

Some of my co-workers were incredulous and asked me why I thought Flash would succeed now, having failed so dismally a few years before, thus resulting in his demise.

I pointed out that the average comic book reader started reading them at the age of eight and gave them up at the age of twelve. And since more than four years had already passed, there was a whole new audience out there who really didn't know that the Flash had flopped, and maybe they might give it a try.

"Good," editorial director Irwin Donenfeld replied, "Now, who will edit it?" All eyes turned to me; thus the former editor of the Golden Age Flash was designated by default as the new editor of the Silver Age Flash.

Four Flash *Showcases* succeeded, and I was given the go-ahead to launch a new series, picking up from that story and continuing on in its own title.

As I started the new series, I had a basic question to confront: Should it be numbered one as the first of the *new* Flash, or should it pick up its numbering from 104 which was where the Golden Age series had left off?

Donenfeld was adamant. It had to be the latter, and when I asked why, he explained. "If you go to a newsstand, you see hundreds of titles on display. If you are looking at two of them side by side and one said number one, and one said number one hundred and four, which is a kid going to spend his hard-earned dime on? If the kid is smart, it will obviously be number one hundred and four and not an unknown number one because any comic that has gone that long must be worth reading."

(This was obviously back in the days prior to the collecting craze that always drove up the inflated prices for back issues that were designated "#1".)

Following the Flash, I successfully revived Green Lantern, the Justice League of America, Hawkman, the Atom, and so on.

When I revived the Atom, I gave him a thorough revamp, as well. The original Atom was Al Pratt, a small, regular person who was exceptionally strong, and I changed him to a hero who could shrink his size down to atomic size (his normal height as a hero would be six inches). I knew he need a civilian identity as well as his secret identity as the Atom, which made me think of my old friend Raymond A. Palmer, who had been the editor at *Amazing Stories* and *Fantastic Adventures*. An accident had damaged his spine when he was a youngster, so Ray never was able to grow to full adult height (or even topping five feet). So I called up Ray and asked his permission to appropriate his name for the civilian identity of the new Atom, and he graciously assented. (An added bonus of the call was that it inspired me to come up with one of the Atom's unique powers, where he could travel from place to place along the phone line as if he was one of the transmitted sound particles.)

Now, one of the innovations I brought to comic-book editing involved a motif that I had picked from my early years as a fan of the pulps. When I was growing up I loved the old dime novels that were published by Street & Smith, particularly those that featured my favorite heroic duo, Frank and Dick Merriwell. There were a whole mess of Merriwell stories that featured Frank or Dick, but it wasn't until they were actually teamed up in a single story that I was completely bowled over.

Individually they were great; together they were *super!*

What a team up!

Another memorable team-up featured the two master villains Rafferty and Chang, who had previously only made solo appearances in *Detective Story* magazine.

I also remember other team-ups, like the time Tarzan went to Pellucidar to help out David Innes, and crossovers between stories, like when it was revealed that Britt Reed (aka the Green Hornet) was descended from Dan Reed (the nephew of the Lone Ranger.

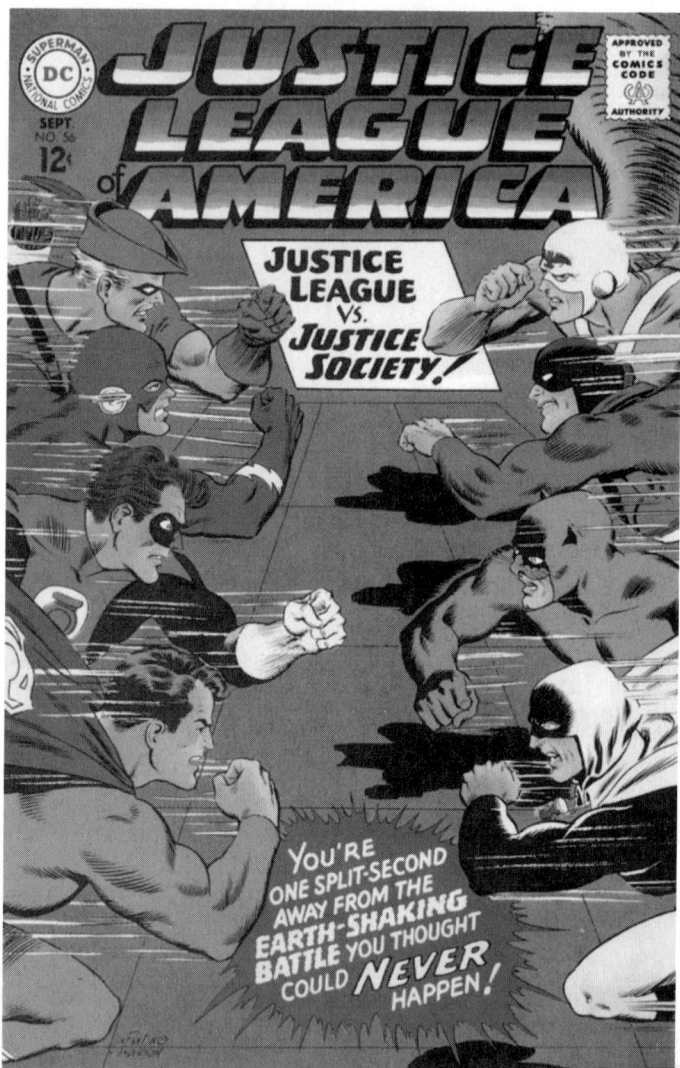

Justice League of America #56, *new heroes versus old.*
(©2000 DC Comics)

Team-ups and crossovers were a great hook, and I frequently used them on the titles I worked on, playing around with different pairings and crossovers. One of the best story ideas that I came up with using this motif was "Flash of Two Worlds."

In the Silver Age Flash series storyline, Barry Allen (aka the Flash) took his superhero name from a super speedster featured in Flash Comics, a series that he had read when he was a kid that featured Jay Garrick of Keystone City, who had superspeed. Thus Allen had modeled himself after his idol, "the Fastest Man on Earth," the Golden Age Flash who even in his fictional reality was also a fictional character.

In "Flash of Two Worlds" (*Flash* #123, September 1961) I allowed Barry Allen to pass into the alternate reality that he thought of as a fictional world by vibrating at superspeed, thus allowing his molecules to pass into the alternate reality that encompassed the same space as our world (remember: I studied physics in college) and actually meet and team up with Jay Garrick. This established a comics precedent of having a character from one universe interact with a character from another universe, the ultimate in crossovers since it was basically Flash meets Flash.

I gave names to the "Two Worlds" of the story's title. I called the world that existed for the current characters in continuity (like Barry Allen) Earth One, and the world of the previous Golden Age characters (such as Jay Garrick) Earth Two. (By the way, those of you currently reading this book inhabit a different Earth, which I had dubbed Earth Prime.) Yeah, I know that from a chronological standpoint, I sort of got it backward, but I wasn't thinking about that until it was way too late to change things.

With the tremendous success of "Flash of Two Worlds" we soon had crossovers galore where Silver Age characters met their Golden Age predecessors or perhaps just did things that couldn't be done in normal continuity (like dying). The high point came with "Crisis on Earth One" (*Justice League of America* #21 and #22) a crossover story between the Earth One heroes of the Justice League of America and the Earth Two heroes of the Justice Society of America. Its tremendous success lead to an annual series of multiple-Earth crossovers, and every possible configuration of collaboration sold well.

A DIFFERENT SORT OF TEAM-UP

Henry Kuttner is perhaps the perfect example of a pulp writer who became extremely proficient at turning out stories by formula and went on to become an extremely prolific and innovative storyteller. I was always impressed with his style, his skill, and his gentlemanliness.

He was also very shy.

C. L. Moore, whose real name was Catherine Lucille Moore (she used the initials quite successfully to conceal her gender in the then-male-oriented field of science fiction an fantasy), was another writer, and one of her most popular characters was Northwest Smith, who adventured on the planet Mars. She also wrote about a character named Jirel of Joiry, a medieval fantasy sword-and-sorcery type of heroine (both characters appeared in Weird Tales).

Kuttner became a fan of Moore's work, particularly the stories featuring these two characters, and decided to write her (thinking her a "him") a letter saying so, care of <u>Weird Tales</u>, one of the magazines in which her stories appeared.

Miss Moore wrote him back, identified herself as Catherine Moore of Indianapolis, and admitted that she was a fan of his work, as well.

Kuttner suggested that perhaps she might consider a crossover story where Smith could meet Jirel, as he thought the two of them would probably really click with each other. Moore thought it was a good idea but admitted that it would be difficult to pull off since they were separated by over forty million miles of space and seven hundred years of time. Kuttner came up with the plot, and the two collaborated on the crossover novel, with each writing alternate chapters, and together they came up with a quite successful story.

On rare occasions Kuttner would drive crosscountry and visit Moore in Indianapolis for a day or so to see his collaborator and pen pal face to face. After about three years of corresponding (and about a total of five days of actually seeing each other spread out over that time), the two decided to get married despite the thousand-mile stretch that separated them geographically because this distance was nothing compared to what they had to overcome to get Jirel of Joiry together with Northwest Smith.

At one point I was asked to help out on *Wonder Woman*. The title was doing poorly, and they had hopes that I would be able to turn it around the way I did *The Flash*.

I did about a year's worth of editorial duty on it, and the gimmick that I came up with to promote and sell it was to have a guest star in every issue. At that time Wonder Woman was not a member of the Justice League. In order to be one, she applied for readmittance, and a Justice League member would guest star in the issue, secretly observing her to decide if she deserved readmittance.

Gardner Fox was a very capable writer.

Not the greatest writer, but very capable and reliable, a good plot man.

In 1944, when I took on the story plotting of the Justice Society of America, I learned of his love for science fiction. I suggested he take a crack at writing for the pulps (still a market, just much smaller by this time), and I would agent the stories for him since I still had an in with most of the editors despite having more or less retired from Solar Sales Service. He took a crack at it and—BANG!—a half a dozen sales to *Planet Stories* and one to *Weird Tales*.

After Fox handed a story in, he would always ask what he could do next. Let's say it was a Justice League story; he'd say, Do you have any ideas? And then the two of us would work out the basics of what the next story should be and iron it out there in the office.

Most important of all, he would always deliver the stories on time.

He brought in a story once, and I noticed that there was a real boner in it. I couldn't believe that he would do a story that had such a big problem and asked him why he had done it that way.

His answer was simple: That was the way we had plotted it! (He never deviated from what his editor exactly instructed.)

Whenever we plotted a story from that point on I would always then send him into the bullpen to type up a one-sheet on what we had discussed that he could show me so we would not make the same sort of bone-headed mistake again.

When I took it upon myself to "Silver Age" the "Golden" Justice Society of America, I changed the name to the Justice League of America. I didn't like Justice Society because it sounded too much like a "club" name like "high society" or something. "Society" was such a quiet word, and the readers were more familiar with "League" from the National League and the American League.

That probably was Gardner's signature work, though he did do a lot of the earlier Justice Society of America stories as well. And later on other writers joined in on his Justice League of America duties.

His wife, Linda, and my wife, Jean, also got along well. He took me to a really good Italian restaurant for a delicious and interesting meal. I was very impressed, and he introduced me to linguini with white clam sauce, which I really liked. It's still a favorite of mine to this day!

He and John Broome were probably the only writers that I socialized with outside of the office.

• • •

After a three-issue tryout in *Brave and Bold* (starting in issue #28), my new Justice League of America debuted in *Justice League* #1 (October/November 1960) with a lineup that featured Flash, Green Lantern, Wonder Woman, J'Onn J'Onzz the Martian Manhunter, and Aquaman, with Batman and Superman scheduled to join the lineup at a later date . . . but then I ran into a slight problem of office politics.

Jack Schiff, who was then the *Batman* editor, and Mort who was then the *Superman* editor, felt that their two heroes might run the danger of becoming overexposed, and together they asked me not to include them in the ongoing Justice League of America series. They could occasionally make a cameo or perhaps a single-issue guest appearance, but they certainly wouldn't appear on the cover.

When the circulation began to slip a little, I went into the publisher to try to come up with some ideas to boost sales. "Gee, I'd like to use Superman and Batman on the cover," I said.

"Why haven't you used them all along?" he demanded.

"Because Mort and Jack didn't want me to," I replied.

"You go in and tell those sonuvabitches that Superman and Batman belong to DC Comics and *not* to Mort Weisinger and Jack Schiff!" he bellowed loudly.

Thus Superman and Batman began to show up on the covers and take part in the adventures, and sales increased dramatically.

Now, my boss who was the head of DC (whose name was Jack Liebowitz) used to play golf with Martin Goodman, who was the head of Marvel Comics, and one day Jack bragged that in addition to beating him at golf, he was also beating him in comics because one of his titles was outselling everything else.

Goodman was incredulous—and scared—and asked what comic that was.

"The *Justice League of America*," Jack replied.

"Never heard of it," Goodman retorted. "What's it about and what's so good about it?"

"Well, instead of having it based around a single superhero, we have a whole team of superheroes working together against a given menace or villain in a booklength adventure, and the kids love it. Quite a novel idea . . . and pretty much every issue is a sellout."

So once the golf game was over, Goodman hightailed it back to his young editor, whose name was Stan Lee, and told him that he wanted him to put out a magazine that featured a group of superheroes working together as a team. And thus was born Marvel's *The Fantastic Four* was born.

(Of course, *The Fantastic Four* sold very well and helped to turn around Marvel's sagging sales, so, do I dare say, indirectly my success with the Justice League of America can be credited with not just saving DC but saving Marvel, as well.) (Nothing like patting ones self on the back, particularly when it is well deserved!)

When it came time to work the old Schwartz editorial magic on Hawkman back in the early sixties, it was obvious to me that the perfect team to accomplish this task was

Gardner Fox and artist Joe Kubert. A Golden Age team was about to be "Silver Aged."

Gardner had written the original Hawkman strip back in the forties, and whereas the original Hawkman was Carter Hall, the reincarnated Egyptian priest Khufu, the new Hawkman would be Carter Hall, aka Katar Hol, a lawman from the planet Thanagar. It's not important who came up with the planet's name, but we all agreed that it was perfect, and if any of us ever discovered a planet, we would probably call it Thanagar.

On plotting days, Gardner came in like clockwork at 10:00 A.M. (usually Monday morning) and we would plot the story in great detail until lunchtime. We'd then finish up, and Gardner would be off to do the script, everything worked out but the actual writing the script itself. I'd give him a deadline for delivery, and he would never miss it.

Joe Kubert was another matter. Very often you got the impression that whatever you saw on the page was burned into Joe's brain before he drew it, and he was just transcribing it tension and all. Joe was the best war-story artist in the business, but his background in superheroes was a bit thin. Notwithstanding this, he was the perfect man for the job.

The new Hawkman/Carter Hall was a classics scholar and a museum curator and expert on all sorts of classical weaponry. And no one could draw fantastic classical weaponry like Joe Kubert.

From a personal note, probably the most important element we added to the mythos was Hawkgirl's sunset-colored hair. Sometime back in the forties, there was a gorgeous gal named Jean Ordwein who came and worked at DC Comics. Everyone wanted to go out with her. Jean had hair the color of sunset, just like Hawkgirl's, and it made a lasting impression on Joe.

At the time Joe was practically still a teenager, but he had a little red sports car, and he sweet-talked Jean into going for rides with him through Central Park. Seeing that Jean was willing to go out with even a kid like Joe helped me to muster up the nerve to ask her out myself.

Joe may have had the first date with Jean, but in time— for all time—I had the rest . . . with Mrs. Jean Schwartz!

Carmine Infantino came up to work at DC (it was still All American Comics then), and he saw Shelly Mayer for an interview. Carmine then came up with Frank Giacoia, who was already doing work for us. Carmine was the penciller, and Frank was the inker (the penciller does the original sketching and drawing of a panel, and the inker goes over the pencil sketch to add definition to the lines and shadows), and Shelly liked their stuff and told me to give them work.

So I gave him a "Ghost Patrol" script to pencil.

When Carmine came in with the job, I remember that he waited for my reaction. I saw that a change was going to be necessary in a certain panel. "Pretty good," I said, "but it needs a fix-up here." He picked it up and went to the corner of the room. He had his back to me, but I still could see that he was sobbing. He had knocked himself out on the assignment and was sure that he had done such a perfect job that I wouldn't be asking for any corrections, and now he

Portrait of the author as a young editor, by Shelly Mayer.
(DC Comics)

thought that he had flunked his assignment. (This was back in about 1945 or 1946.)

Giacoia was a superb inker, and I recall that they did many great stories together. Frank never did any pencils for me. I think he did most of his work for the syndicates on such strips as *Sherlock Holmes*, maybe with Mike Sekowsky, who did a lot of ghosting.

Mike was faster than the proverbial *two* speeding bullets when it came to inking.

My best story about Mike Sekowsky is when he used to be my premier artist on the Justice League, and years later he was given an Inkpot Award. As he passed me at the ceremony he pointed a finger at me and said, "This means a raise, you know."

Also, Mike used to like to have a drink with lunch on occasion. When he was doing Justice League for me I remember once when I had to tell him, "Mike, you have to do the cover today, so when you come back from lunch you have to be prepared to do the cover. So no more than two martinis for lunch."

. . . and on occasion when Mike didn't come back from lunch, I had to summon someone else (usually Murphy Anderson) to pitch in on the work that was on deadline.

Carmine, on the other hand, was always very reliable. He usually pencilled at least two full pages a day, and he would often do that work in the office. I understand it was part of his normal routine that on the next day he would look at the two pages he had done on the previous day, and if he didn't like them he would tear them up and start again and do those two pages plus two more pages before finishing for the day.

He was a harsh judge of his own work.

Carmine was an impressionist when it came to backgrounds. I remember poor Murphy, with whom he worked on the Adam Strange comics—Carmine would just lightly pencil to suggest the backgrounds, and Murphy would have to sharpen the details during his inking. (Murphy would always try to work in a different part of the office from

Carmine so that Carmine wouldn't see what he was doing. When Carmine would come to look over his shoulder, Murphy would turn the page over and doodle on it so that Carmine couldn't get a look at it.)

Carmine was also not particularly good at anatomy consistency and sometimes Murphy would have to work it out and fix it during the inking stage.

Carmine's biggest anatomical problem was that in drawing he could never tell his right from his left. Let me explain. A right-handed gunfighter would keep his gun and holster on the right side, and if he came to a door and turned around, the gun-side would now appear to be on the left, but Carmine would frequently mix it up, and the holster would wind up alternating sides, even though the shooter was supposed to be right-handed.

On *Batman*, Carmine was inconsistent with the number of packets and holders on Batman's utility belt. He may not have paid attention to the little details . . . but he was great on everything else, and at the time he was my number-one artist.

Basically, he was wonderful.

It was rumored that Carmine let management know that after a time he would only continue to work for DC as long as his rate was at least a dollar more than anyone else's. (I seem to also remember that Gil Kane went in and demanded the same rate as Carmine, and when he didn't get it, he decided to go to work for Marvel for a while instead.)

Carmine's signature works were probably Adam Strange and his work on the Silver Age Flash (Barry Allen) and a lot of my science fiction.

• • •

At one point I wanted to use Carmine exclusively on *Batman,* but at the time Bob Kane had a contract or some other agreement where he had to be offered every other job on *Detective Comics,* and the others would be done by Carmine. But that didn't last forever.

He did a lot of science fiction for me. I remember he did Captain Comet. He was actually the first new super-hero of the 1950s, and it may not have started the Silver Age, but when all of the heroes had died out except for Superman, Batman, and Wonder Woman, Captain Comet made his debut in *Strange Adventures* #9 in June 1951. I remember I used a word to describe him that Marvel Comics would later use for a lot of their characters. I called him a "mutant," a man born one hundred thou-sand years ahead of his time (predating Marvel's mutants by years).

Carmine did the originals for that incarnation of Captain Comet, and Murphy Anderson took it over eventually. Carmine also did a lot of westerns—*Johnny Thunder,* I think—and he also did *Detective Chimp* and *Rex the Wonder Dog* (both with scripts by John Broome) . . . but he was pretty terrible on horses . . . and, lest we forget, *Strange Sports* stories!

I remember one day Carmine came to me and said that he wanted to be invited to the next editorial meeting. I asked why, and he said that he wanted to talk to them about something. So I asked whoever—Irwin Donenfeld, I believe—was running the meeting if it was all right and he said sure, and I told Carmine it would be ok and when the next meeting was.

At the meeting Irwin asked Carmine why he wanted to be there.

Carmine explained that he had taken an entire month's worth of DC covers and did them over *his* way and here they were. And he passed them around.

Everyone had to agree that Carmine's versions were better than the ones that DC was currently using, so—and now I have to just speculate because I don't really know what Irvin said to him—I have to assume that at that point he was made the equivalent of a cover editor . . . and that's how he got started on his way to the executive suite, from whence he eventually ran the entire company.

Carmine realized that he wasn't *really educated* in the sense of formal schooling. He had attended a school for industrial art but not an academic high school or college or anything, so one day he came in and asked me to put together a list of twenty books for him, those that every well-educated person should have read.

He was aware of his shortcomings and always tried to better himself.

Even as an executive Carmine always maintained control of the covers. He would do the layout and the sketch, and then he would give the sketch to Nick Cardy, the artist, to flesh out, and Nick would bring in the cover. I remember one time Carmine raised holy hell because Nick hadn't followed his sketch, so he immediately fired Nick.

I asked him who was going to do the covers now that he had fired Nick.

Carmine thought for a moment and snapped back at me to immediately get Nick back in so he could rehire him.

DÉJÀ VU ALL OVER AGAIN!

Its amazing how history repeats itself.

One of the things that I did in the letter columns of the series that I edited was print the addresses of the correspondents. I remembered how my first introduction to other fans was through the letter columns of the early science-fiction magazines. This was how I started corresponding with other fans and authors and, as I previously explained, how fandom basically came about in the science-fiction field.

Well, it was déjà vu all over again in the field of comics.

Two fans by the names of Roy Thomas and Jerry Bails started to correspond with each other after having read each other's mail in my columns. (Both had already taken to corresponding with me very actively—in fact, they wrote so much that occasionally I would have to use pseudonyms in place of their names in the columns; their letters were that good that I really wanted to run them, and at the same time, I didn't want everyone to think that Jerry and Roy were our only two fans.) Their correspondence led to their collaboration on the fanzine Alter Ego (shades of Mort and me and The Time Traveller), which eventually led to conventions that were

*The Masters of Comics Fandom. From left: Don Thompson,
Steve Geppi, Maggie Thompson, yours truly, Paul Levitz, and
Roy Thomas at the 1991 presentation of the Gem Award by
Diamond Comic Distributors, Inc.*

held exclusively for comics fans and professionals
(rather than as a minority group at science-fiction
conventions) . . . and once again the rest is history!

So, not just satisfied to be one of the founding
members of science-fiction fandom, I can also claim the
honor of having been a seminal part of the founding of
comics fandom, as well!

On one occasion Mort asked me what I knew about Roy
Thomas, and I told him that as I recall he was going to be
a school teacher (he was already an editor of a fanzine by
the name of *Alter Ego*, which I wholeheartedly endorsed),
and he was coming to the Washington D.C. area for some
reason from the St. Louis area. Why? I asked.

MAN OF TWO WORLDS

Well, as it turned out, Mort was looking for replacement for his assistant Nelson Bridwell and he was considering hiring Roy.

So Mort called him in and hired him.

As I recall, Roy didn't really enjoy working for Mort, and on one lunch hour he hurried over to Marvel Comics and took their writing test—they gave you a page, and you had to fill in the balloons right there on the spot—and evidently Stan Lee liked what he saw and offered him a job.

Roy came back, gave his notice, and went over to Marvel.

Roy Thomas could certainly talk, nonstop, hardly ever taking a breath.

I remember one time he called me up to discuss a story we were working on, and he just got talking and talking, and I couldn't get a word in edgewise. Eventually I put the phone down on my desk and went out to the "Bat-room" (bathroom), and when I came back I picked up the phone—and sure enough, Roy was still talking and hadn't even noticed that I had figuratively put him on hold for a few minutes.

I like to think that for the most part I got along well with all of my writers. I was "Mr. Reliable"—I always tried to keep the work coming their way and always tried to have the check on hand when they came into deliver their assignment rather than having them wait to be paid on their next trip in.

Sometimes, though, you just can't please everyone. Let's consider the case of Alex Toth.

Alex Toth was still a high school student when he brought in his portfolio of samples to be reviewed by Shelly Mayer, who liked what he saw and sent him down the hallway to my office for an assignment.

Both Shelly and I agreed: Alex's work was extraordinary! I gave him an assignment, he did it, and I went over it with Shelly. We both decided that he had made the grade, so I continued to feed him assignments.

I distinctly remember that on certain occasions his work would be dropped off or his check and assignment would be picked up by his mother. I gave him some work in *Strange Adventures* (some science-fiction stuff) and a few *Johnny Thunder* stories plus probably a few assignments on other titles that I was responsible for.

On one particular occasion, instead of going out to lunch, I ordered my lunch in so that I could play a round of two-handed bridge with one of my co-workers over the lunch hour (I might have wanted to eat in because it was raining out or maybe I just needed a "bridge fix" to feed my habit). And during my lunch hour Alex came by early with his assignment and wanted me to accept the work and give him his check and next assignment so that he could be on his way.

I explained that I was at lunch and in the middle of a game and that I would be finished in about ten or fifteen minutes, and instructed him to go take a seat in my office, and I would be with him shortly.

I finished the game and my lunch in about the time I had projected, and went back to my office to meet with Alex.

As per usual, Alex's work was beautiful, and though I planned on giving it a closer look later, I passed him the check and told him that it was a job well done. I then gave him his next assignment.

Now, at this point we had a disagreement. I had two assignments lined up for him—we'll call them A and B. He wanted to do *B* first, but deadlines dictated that I needed *A* first.

"Oh, no!" he exclaimed. "My next assignment isn't *Strange Adventures*, it's *Johnny Thunder*!"

"No! It's *Strange Adventures*," I thundered.

Alex insisted, "*Johnny Thunder* or nothing!"

I figured I could dig in just as easily as he could and answered, "Fine, you can do nothing, then." I had just thrown it in, assuming that he would back down, and everything would proceed on schedule.

Alex grumbled, then left the office assignmentless. He didn't work for me again for quite a while (though he did continue working for other editors at DC).

Twenty-five years later I am at San Diego Comic Convention to receive my Inkpot Award (presented to me by Ray Bradbury), and a bearded character walks by me, does a double-take, and turns around and says, "Boss? Boss?"

"Alex? Alex?" I reply, and we embrace. All was forgiven.

Very soon after, the relationship repaired, he took on another assignment from me—not a *Strange Adventures* or a *Johnny Thunder* story but a *Superman-Batman* story.

Another time in the mid-seventies, a writer by the name of Jim Shooter (who would later achieve a degree of fame—or perhaps infamy—at Marvel) became dissatisfied with the treatment that he was receiving from me and the two editors working under me, Nelson Bridwell and Bob Rozakis, and drafted a one and a half page letter to Carmine complaining about us.

Carmine, of course, just sent Jim's letter back to me for reply.

I wrote:

> My dear fellow—JS:
> You pulled a BIG BLOOPER sending this to CI—ALMOST as big as the mistake you made in your splash having FLASH "turn around and go home" just because SUPERMAN can't knock out that criminal.
> Au contraire—FLASH would rather FIGHT than FLIGHT!
> For the last and final time ///
>
> JS.

And he never wrote for me again, which at the time I didn't really consider to be much of a loss for DC or myself. But time heals all wounds (I know, I know, it's not original!), and Jim and I socialized after a while.

Straining my neck looking up at his six-foot-six frame,

I'd kiddingly tell him not to wear those narrow ties of his because they made him look even taller.

"Go for a wide tie!" I insisted. "A wide tie will make a Shooter shorter!"

Sure enough, the next time I saw Jim Shooter, he flipped his newly acquired wide tie at me with a smile.

PART FOUR

BATMAN, SUPERMAN, AND COMICS COME OF AGE

I was never given credit as editor in the indicia of the comic books I worked on until early 1959—probably about the time Whit went out to California about the various TV series projects that were in development, ranging from cartoons to the phenomenally successful *Batman* series.

At the time the only editorial credit went to Whit Ellsworth as editor in chief. One day Mort, Jack Schiff, and I decided to ask to be credited in the issues as editor for the titles/series that we did. After all, we were the ones doing the work, and we were the ones answering readers' letters for the given titles.

Whit got back to us very quickly, and—*poof!*—we had editorial credit.

When I first got involved with *Batman.* I wasn't really interested in that stories. I was more interested in the science-fiction stories that I was working on with Adam Strange, Green Lantern, etc., but editorial director Irwin Donenfeld (the son of Harry Donenfeld, the original president and founder of DC Comics) said that I had to take over *Batman*, and so I did.

Sounds simple . . . well not really.

I loved science fiction! It was the real reason I wanted to be an editor, and I even worked with the writers who I had read and agented to the science-fiction magazines. Ed Hamilton had scripted several stories for me, including "The Micro-men" (*Mystery in Space* #2) and "The Man With Four Minds" (*Strange Adventures* #69), Henry Kuttner contributed "Time to Kill" (*Phantom Stranger* #5), and Otto Binder had done numerous assignments including "The Great Space-Train Robbery" (*Mystery in Space* #19), "The Gorilla World" (*Strange Adventures* #45), and "Robinson Crusoe of Space" (*Mystery in Space* #30), not to mention my stalwart stable of scripters like John Broome, Gardner Fox, and Eddie Herron, who made each issue of my science-fiction comics a joy to read.

All told, from 1950 to 1964 I had edited over 160 issues of *Strange Adventures* and over 90 issues of *Mystery in Space.*

. . . but the boss wanted me to take over *Batman* to save it, and there are some powers that even the gods on Earth have to obey.

• • •

Before I took over, *Batman* had become more of a science-fiction take-off piece with robots and aliens all over the place, and I really hadn't been following the continuity. Thus the first story of my *Batman* tenure had a big mistake in it that I didn't notice. I had asked my top writer at the time, John Broome, to do the job, and he more or less seemed to have shared the same lack of excitement for Bob Kane's creation as I did. So the two of us sat down together and carefully plotted a story for the Caped Crusader that was set in the Gotham City equivalent of Greenwich Village (complete with a Jefferson Square Park and arch to compliment New York's Washington Square Park and arch).

There we were, two professionals not realizing that when it came to *Batman* we were the blind leading the blind.

The story was titled "Mystery of the Menacing Mask" (*Detective Comics* #327), and the mistake was that at the story's climax Batman holds a gun on the crooks—and as everyone familiar with the book was quick to point out, this was something Batman would never do.

A SUPER BLOOPER

There was a wonderful mistake in the <u>Superman</u> TV series that was always repeated and never picked up on, and it's one of those things that goes from being dumb to being really dumb right before your eyes.

Invariably in any given episode, Superman—as played by George Reeves—would break down a wall or fly in and surprise the crooks, who would immediately recognize him as Superman. The crooks would then proceed to shoot their guns empty as we viewers would watch the bullets bounce off his chest. (Mistake number one: If they knew he was Superman, they should have known that bullets would just bounce off him.) Once they were out of bullets, the crooks would inevitably throw their guns at him. (Mistake number two: If the bullets didn't hurt him, what could have lead them to believe that throwing the guns would have any effect?!) The crowning touch was of course Reeves's reaction to the entire scene where he would boldly take the shots squarely in the chest with a superior smile on his face—but would then duck when they threw the guns at him. Superman may have been invincible, but I guess George Reeves was a bit wary at having even an empty piece of metal thrown at him.)

As I became more acquainted with the Batman character and his legacies, I realized that I was going to have to make a few changes, much in the same way that I did when I had taken over other established characters. By my estimation, the Batman in the years prior to my tenure had strayed away from the original roots of the character.

Batman was regarded as the world's greatest detective, so I decided that he should return to his dark-mystery roots. Likewise, he was also a great escape artist, so I decided to bring back the trap motifs that Bill Finger had done so well during the early years (many of the most popular covers would feature Batman in some sort of death trap, and the thrust of the issue would wind up being how he got there and how he got out).

I just couldn't believe that he'd be going down into the Batcave on a winding staircase, so I had an elevator installed, an automatic secret garage door entrance/exit for the Batcave, and I also souped up the Batmobile. (There were also references to that very hip "hootenanny" music that was then very popular with the young people.)

And to set off for history the start of my term as editor on the title, I had them incorporate an oval around the bat emblem on Batman's chest, so there would never be any question as to when the Julie Schwartz *Batman* came into being, heralded by a banner logo across the top of my first issue, proudly proclaiming

INTRODUCING A "NEW LOOK"
BATMAN AND ROBIN IN "MYSTERY OF THE MENACING MASK"

(Yes, the story with the blooper in it!).

I also replaced the second feature of the issue, which had been stories featuring John Jones the Manhunter from Mars (which moved to *House of Mystery* which former *Batman* editor Jack Schiff would continue to edit) with the Elongated Man, who had previously appeared in *Flash* comics (heralded by an insert of a *Flash* cover depicting both Flash and Kid Flash wishing him good luck on his new solo adventures in *Detective Comics*). At this point in time the Elongated Man was a bit of a novelty because he was the only superhero to have publicly revealed his true identity.

Though I was allowed to make some changes to the *Batman* series, there was at least one thing that I was forbidden to change. The easiest way to reinvent a comic series without actually changing the identity of the hero (as we did during the renovation of Green Lantern and the Flash) is to change the artist on the series. But per Bob Kane's agreement with DC, about half of the *Batman* titles were contracted to him for illustration. (This was also the first time someone other than Bob Kane received credit in any creative capacity for *Batman*.)

Now, it was common knowledge that Bob had made arrangements with Shelly Moldoff to ghost most of his illustrating work at the time, but nevertheless we continued with the charade of working with Bob as if he actually did the work.

But there was one particular time when even Bob had to admit the reality of the situation.

A script had come in, and I had set up a meeting with Bob in order to pass on some specific instructions with the assignment. Marvel had begun experimenting with certain altered perspectives in their graphic storytelling that gave the effect of a sort of 3-D look as if a punch was jumping right off the page. It was the Jack Kirby look, where the action violated the frame for added impact. I showed some samples to Bob and instructed him that a certain panel would be perfect for this sort of effect. He agreed, accepted the assignment, and took it back to his studio.

At the appointed time of deadline, Bob returned to the office with the assignment. I gave it a quick review and immediately noticed that he (in reality Shelly) had failed to do as I had instructed on that panel. I pointed it out to Bob, he nodded, recalling our conversation (having probably forgotten to tell Shelly about it), and offered to fix it at one of the spare desks in the artists' bullpen.

A little while later he returned with his handiwork, and it was horrible, worse than anything I had seen in a long time. I was polite but firm and informed him that it wouldn't do. Yet again, he agreed with me and said he would fix it, then headed back to the bullpen.

Yet another little while later he returned, and this time the panel was perfect . . . but I couldn't understand why there was such a big discrepancy between this one and the previous one.

Bob revealed that Murphy Anderson was at the desk next to the one he had worked at, and on the second time around he decided to ask Murphy to do it for him. And as usual Murphy had done an excellent job. It was exactly what I wanted.

I gave Bob the check for the assignment but decided that I had to press the point a little and asked him why he had Murphy do it instead of doing it himself.

His reply shocked me.

"Three little words:" he answered, "lack . . . of . . . talent."

Now, at the time that I was asked to take over *Batman*, DC had already taken a lot of heat from Dr. Fredric Wertham with his book *Seduction of the Innocent*. Wertham maintained that comics were harmful to kids, and one of the things that came up was about how "unnatural" the living arrangements were at Wayne manor—what he construed as basically a household of three unmarried males—and the self-proclaimed expert raised unfounded questions about what might really be going on.

So I decided to bring a woman into the household, a spinster aunt of Dick "Robin" Grayson, who could possibly be seen as a sort of chaperoning den mother. Her name was Aunt Harriet—taken from the old Hoagy Carmichael song "Rockin' Chair," where he talks about his old Aunt Harriet wherever she may be—and to provide the excuse for this, I decided that I would have Alfred the butler killed off.

Now, I probably could have brought a woman into the mix some other way—a marriage, a sister, another ward, or something—but, honestly, the first idea that crossed my mind was to kill off Alfred. And as was usual for me, my first inclination always seemed to be the best way to go.

I knew that the perfect person to do the story would be the person who had created Alfred in the first place—namely, Bill Finger.

We decided to kill Alfred at the cost of his own life saving Batman in some situation, and I heralded this in the letter column in *Detective* #327:

We're going out on a limb with our prediction that next issue's "Gotham Gang Line Up" will stir up more excitement and controversy than any Batman story ever published! To keep you in suspense, we shall refrain from dropping the slightest hint about the dramatic development to be unfolded in this history-making yarn.

"Invigorated by our "new look" policy, Bob Kane— Batman's originator—has fashioned an extraordinary art job for "Gotham Gang Line Up" inspired by the swell script of Bill Finger, who has written many of the *classic* Batman adventures of the past two decades.

Pretty exciting, huh?

I also decided to bring back some of Bill Finger's great villains that had been neglected in recent years, with such stories as "The Joker's Comedy Capers!" scripted by John Broome and "The Riddle-less Robberies of the Riddler" scripted by Gardner Fox (*Batman* #171).

We also spent a lot of time coming up with great new traps to bedevil the Caped Crusader, such as "The Castle with Wall to Wall Danger" (*Detective* #329) and "The Two Way Death Trap" (*Batman* #166). I used to have a lot of fun plotting some of these with Gardner Fox. We would come up with the trap in the morning and then try to solve it. If we couldn't solve it by lunch, we would eat out together, then come back and solve it. (I confess that I would often solve the trap prior to lunch but hold back till the afternoon so that we would have to have our lunch date with Gardner picking up the tab.) To further boost the "detective" side of the *Batman* books, I occasionally added a second feature back-up story to issues spotlighting a gentlemen's club called "The Mystery Analysts of Gotham City" (introduced in *Batman* #164), where you could only become a member if you actually solved a mystery.

I would challenge the readers to try to solve the mystery with the members by spotting the clues along the way. (In retrospect, these stories seem quite similar in theme to those that Isaac Asimov wrote as his *Tales of the Black Widowers* . . .

but he didn't even start them until close to ten years after I introduced the Mystery Analysts. I wonder . . .)

DAVE VERN

There was an idea for one *Batman* story that came to me in the middle of the night. It was called "Where Were You On the Night Batman Was Killed?" (<u>Batman</u> #291–294).

The idea was that Batman was missing, and Catwoman, the Joker, Riddler, and Lex Luthor (yet another crossover) each claim that they did it, and the case is eventually tried by Bruce Wayne.

The story was by Dave Vern, who wrote as David V. Reed.

Much earlier in our careers, Dave Vern introduced me to Dixieland jazz, and I introduced him to Ray Palmer (the editor of <u>Amazing Stories</u>, not the Atom). Dave went to work for him in Chicago. Feeling homesick, he then convinced Ray to let him have an office in New York since all of the stories were bought by Julius Schwartz anyway, who was, of course back in New York, thus allowing him direct contact with the lead literary agent in the field.

Dave was a rabid Brooklyn Dodgers fan, and on the occasion when an afternoon game was being broadcast on the radio, Dave, while manuscript reading, would also be baseball listening with the radio turned down really low . . . and he didn't like to be interrupted.

Invariably, mid-game there would come a knocking at the door . . . which Dave, of course, chose to ignore.

On one occasion the knocking persisted, with

subsequent knocks getting louder and louder. With the stealth of a cat burglar, Dave tiptoed to the door and looked through the keyhole to see who was rap, rap, rapping and interrupting his afternoon routine.

His inside eye caught sight of an outside eye looking back a him, framed by the keyhole.

Opening the door, he came face to face with the one person he really wanted to avoid . . . the writer, Ray Cummings, with a manuscript firmly in hand.

Cummings (a veteran science-fiction author from the early years of the field) had had story after story rejected by Dave and was itching for a confrontation, which, of course, got Cummings nowhere, as usual. Dave accepted the submission, and shortly thereafter sent it back to Cummings with its traditional rejection letter, as usual.

Alfred Bester once said, "Dave Vern is a much better writer than me."

Roughly around this time, a gentleman about to take an airplane flight had nothing to read, and he happened to pick up an issue that I had edited. He enjoyed the Batman story and particularly enjoyed the villain of the piece, who was the Riddler. The stories, characters, and ideas excited him, and he tracked down another previous issue that featured the Joker. This gentleman's name was William Dozier, and he set in motion the deals that brought about the *Batman* TV show, with himself as the producer.

Unfortunately, at about the same time that they were going about adapting Batman to television, William Dozier

had recently renewed his familiarity with the cast of characters by reading the stories featuring the Joker, Catwoman,
and the Riddler—which provided the inspiration for three
of the scripts. Dozier decided that there were a few changes
that I had made that he wasn't too thrilled with.

Foremost of all, Dozier insisted Alfred be part of the
ongoing TV continuity, and so he contacted DC and told
them to bring the butler back.

Fortunately at that time I ran a series of stories featuring
a supernatural character called the Outsider, who was
inspired by the title of an old H. P. Lovecraft story, and by
brainstorming it with Gardner Fox, we worked out a way to
reveal that the Outsider was really Alfred the butler—thus
enabling us to quite literally bring him back from the dead
no worse the wear.

After the TV series had been on for about a year, Dozier
decided that we needed to do something new to hype the
program, and he asked if there was any way that we could
add a young female as an ongoing cast member.

I asked what kind of girl he had in mind, and as it turned
out he had already worked out a possible scenario in his
head whereby Commissioner Gordon had a daughter who
decides to become Batgirl. So Gardner Fox and I went back
to the office and created Batgirl in a story entitled "The
Million Dollar Debut of Batgirl" in *Detective Comics* #359
and she was then written into the program.

Years later I had the pleasure of meeting the very
attractive actress Yvonne Craig, who played Barbara
"Batgirl" Gordon, who seemed quite appreciative of my

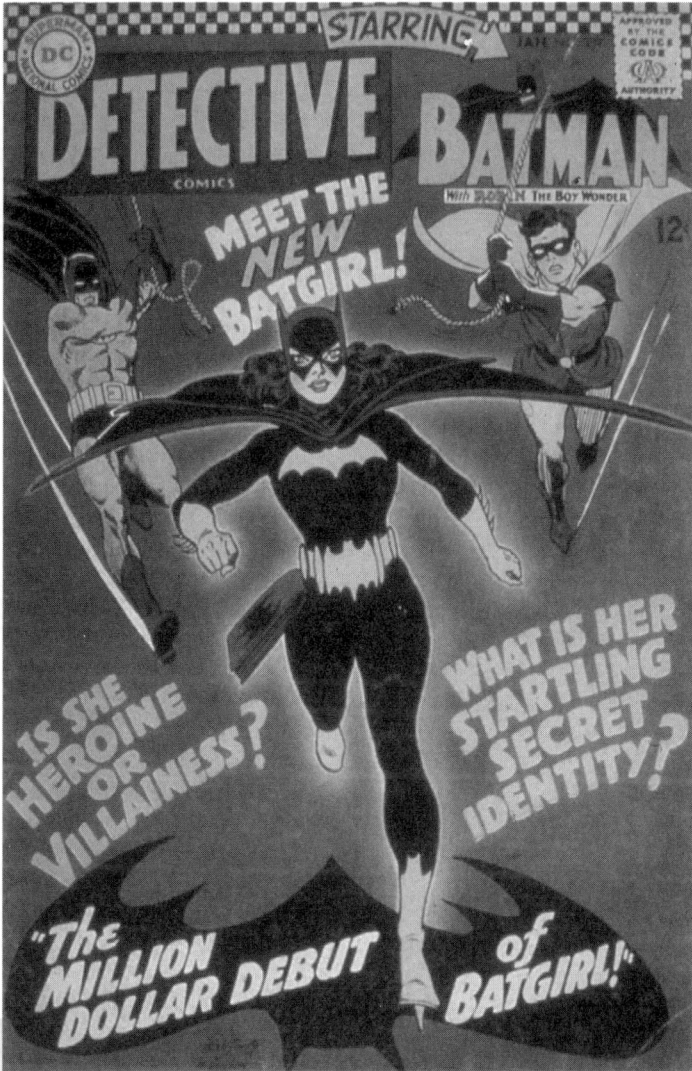

Detective Comics #359—*presenting Batgirl!* (©2000 DC
Comics)

The real Batgirl, Yvonne Craig, shows her appreciation for a devoted fan. (Beth Gwinn)

part in her character's creation, and she rewarded me with a kiss.

As always, I was also on the lookout for exciting new villains who could bedevil the Caped Crusaders, and artist Neal Adams and scripter Denny O'Neil came up with a worthy adversary with deductive faculties to rival the master detective. This mysterious figure possessed a warped sense of moral authority, an exotic background out of the Far East, and, with a nod toward my returning Batman to his master detective roots, a propensity for addressing Batman as "Detective."

The story was entitled "Daughter of the Demon" in *Batman* #232, and it was in the vein of a classic detective story, complete with reader access to the same clues as Batman so that the mystery could be solved along with the master detective himself.

Artistically, Neal came up with the look of Ra's Al Ghul, but I came up with the idea for the character.

I was reading in an astronomy book and came across the fact that an *algol* star is called "demon star" and gets its name from the Arabic or the Semitic equivalent *al ghul*, which means a ghoul, and *raz* from the Hebrew meaning "head." Thus *raz al ghul* is the head of the demons (ghouls).

Denny fleshed out the character's background and manner and made him real. He wrote a really classic series of stories that built to a mystical crescendo, with Neal doing a terrific job of illustrating them.

UNSOLICITED EXCELLENCE

There are only two times in my entire career in comics that I can ever recall going with a story that was an over-the-transom submission—that is, a complete story that was not solicited and approved in advance of it being written. Normally, since schedules are worked out in advance and plot lines and story arcs are so complicated, it is pretty near impossible for someone to do an adequate job without access to all the appropriate information.

Elliot Maggin was a student at Brandeis University, and for a term project for his American social history course, he did a script for a Green Arrow story entitled "What Can One Man Do?" After receiving his grade and credit for it, he decided to send it in to me. It was a little too long for our needs (and would therefore have to be trimmed back a bit), but I couldn't believe that it was so good—particularly from an unknown.

I handed it around the office for some reassurances, asking, "Read this story and tell me if it is as good as I think it is."

Everyone agreed with my opinion and thought that we should schedule it as soon as possible. By some chance it fell into the hands of Neal Adams, who read it, liked it, and insisted, "No one is doing this story but me."

And he did—with the exception of a single page (the opening "splash page") that we never got around to inking since he handed the pencils in so late, forcing us to shoot the pencil sketches instead since an inked version did not exist.

The story ran in Green Lantern/Green Arrow #87 (December 1971/January 1972)

(Elliot, by the way, went on to a prolific career in comics, authored the New York Times bestselling Superman novel The Last Son of Krypton, and even ran for Congress.)

(The other unsolicited success story was the case of a fellow who was a graduate of the Joe Kubert school of art — the same Joe Kubert who as a teenager took my then-to-be wife for a ride through Central Park. His name was Craig Boldman, and he wrote a Superman story that featured Jimmy Olsen.)

Now, Neal Adams's and my memories disagree on the way a lot of things happened.

Case in point—Man-Bat.

I distinctly recall I was plotting in the office, and I was sitting there with Frank Robbins. We were trying to come up with a new villain for Batman when it occurred to me that our problem could be solved by just reversing the words bat and man and coming up with Man-Bat . . . and that was the beginning of it, and he did the rest of the plotting and the writing and so on.

Neal claims he was sitting in the office and that *he* suggested the idea of a "manbat" . . . but that's not how I remember it. As I recall it, he wasn't there until later, after Frank had worked it all out.

RELEVANT COMICS

It was also during this period of time that we tried a daring experiment. The old guard of the early Silver Age was being replaced by the new guard that was coming of age in the sixties. One of the hot new talents was a writer from the Midwest by the name of Denny O'Neil, who was working with a hot young artist by the name of Neal Adams.

A segment of the professional comics community as well as of the readership thought that comics should come of age much the same way American society was in the social revolution of the 1960s. Racial strife, the antiwar movement, and the drug abuse crisis were all part of the American scene as witnessed each evening on the nightly news . . . but did these issues belong in comics? And the even bigger question, could comics become relevant?

Denny and Neal were chomping at the bit, and we were about to find out.

At the time the <u>Green Lantern</u> title was dying (the previous Schwartz revitalization now a part of a more-than-decade-old past), and a decision was made to use it as our proving ground to expand the comics medium, examine its boundaries, and explore a new realm—namely, relevance and realism. Businesswise it wasn't much of a gamble since the title was already on its last legs. And who knew? Perhaps an injection of relevance might save it.

Denny and Neal teamed the Green Lantern, Hal Jordan, with the Green Arrow, Oliver Queen, in a series of <u>Green Lantern/Green Arrow</u> adventures that dealt directly with the tough issue of racism in America by putting a spotlight on the discrimination and prejudice issue that had been all but absent from comics up to that point—complete with lyric excerpts from the poet laureate of relevance, Bob Dylan.

(One particularly memorable scene in the award-winning story "No Evil Shall Escape My Sight" featured an elderly black man who questioned the two heroes why they had no trouble spending their time saving multicolored aliens on other worlds but never seemed to get around to doing anything for blacks on Earth.)

A subsequent story line featured Green Arrow discovering that his young sidekick, Speedy, a comic book junior hero in his own right, had become a drug addict right under his own nose, disproving the false notion that only someone else's kid uses drugs.

The verdict was soon in.

Older readers went wild over the story lines and praised the books. Both Denny and Neal won numerous awards for their groundbreaking work. It was a critical success, it didn't lose money, and it gained DC a lot of favorable publicity. But the younger readers (who still made up the majority of the readership) didn't want relevance, they wanted entertainment—and for them the two did not match up, so eventually we had to let the the the <u>Green Lantern/Green Arrow</u> series die. It had served its purpose, and new ground had been broken. The revamped series lasted a total of thirteen issues plus an additional twenty-four pages of story line that continued past the series cancellation as a second feature in <u>Flash,</u> which I also edited.

Every year or so Mort would tell our boss Jack Liebowitz that he wanted to retire, and Jack (he always wanted us to call him Jack) would talk him out of it.

Then one day in 1970, (surprise! surprise!) he accepted the resignation since he himself was leaving DC. I was asked to take over *Superman* (the way they had "asked" me to take over *Batman*). I warned them that I would want to change things around, the way I had when I took over *Green Lantern* and *Batman*.

Needless to say, the higher-ups were a little worried, not wanting me to interfere too much with a proven commodity, and asked me what sort of changes I had in mind.

The first thing I wanted to do concerned his strength. I wanted to reduce his powers a bit. So where during Mort's editorship Supes was able to hold the world up on the tip of one finger, under my tutelage he would have to use both hands.

I also wanted to get rid of all of the kryptonite that kept turning up. Whenever Mort needed to juice up the suspense, the crooks would get a hold on some kryptonite to threaten Superman, and I felt that the old green rock of death was just getting tired.

THE TRUE STORY OF
THE ORIGIN OF KRYPTONITE

Kryptonite was not originally part of the whole Superman story line in the comics and was in fact brought to the story line due to something that happened on the Superman radio show.

Bud Collier—who would later go on to host To Tell the Truth—was the voice of Superman. The show was very popular, and Collier's voice was easily recognized.

One day Collier came in and let everyone know that he wouldn't see them for two weeks because he was taking his vacation as was guaranteed by his contract.

Now, radio was done live in those days, and the producers of the show were immediately thrown into a state of panic on what they were going to do for two weeks until Collier returned. They quickly concocted a plot involving a deadly rock of kryptonite that a criminal got a hold of and managed to trap Superman in a room with it, where he was rendered powerless and greatly weakened.

For the next two weeks of story, amazing Superman was trapped in that room moaning his lines weakly, almost unrecognizable because of the debilitating effects of the rock.

Two weeks later Collier returned, a rejuvenated Superman escaped—his strength returned—and his voice was brought back to normal.

And so kryptonite entered the canon of Superman mythos forever.

Likewise, I wanted to get rid of the robots that Superman always used to fill in for himself (or Clark Kent) to enable them both to appear in one place at the same time. It was just too easy.

Schwartz and Kent, editor and reporter.

I also wanted to change Clark Kent's wardrobe and give it a snazzier, more modern look. At the time, he was always wearing that same cockamamie blue suit, so I made sure that from then on he was dressed at the height of fashion—so much so that *Gentleman's Quarterly*, the fashion magazine for men, did an article on him and his new look. There was even an interview with scripter Denny O'Neil on the *Today* show.

Most importantly of all, I decided that Clark had to leave the *Daily Planet*. Young people didn't relate to newspaper reporters. They got their news from the television, so therefore it was only natural that Clark Kent should take a job as a television reporter.

I would always put him on location for remote broadcasts, and if all of a sudden a plane started to fall out of the sky, he would announce that it was time to go back to the studio for a commercial—and off camera by the time the commercial was over, the plane and its passengers were saved, and Clark Kent had a new story to report right on the scene.

On one occasion, the news editor was holding up a chalkboard that indicated that there were sixty seconds left in the broadcast when Clark saw a critical situation that demanded Superman's attention. So he altered the chalk marks with his heat vision to six seconds and signed off, changed in the stockroom, and saved the day while the editor stood there scratching his head, wondering how he could have gotten the timing all wrong.

I also gave him a foil by the name of Steve Lombard, a sports jock at the station who teased Clark mercilessly, calling him namby-pamby, nerd, etc., just to make Clark's life a bit less comfortable and a bit more interesting.

(Finally, as a sort of inside joke that would maintain a spiritual continuity, we added a piece of sculpture to Clark's apartment. It was a classical bust of what appeared to be a dignified gentleman. Whenever Clark would go home, he would take off his hat and toss onto the head of the bust saying, "Evening Morty." A close examination of the bust's visage would always reveal a certain distinct similarity to that of my predecessor, Mort Weisinger.)

Now, one of my biggest problems with taking over the *Superman* editorial duties was my unfamiliarity with everything that had gone before in the comic (1938–1970). Sure I knew the basics, the mythos, the villains, and other characters, but Mort had been the editor for close to thirty years, and that was a lot of history to cover.

Lucky for me, my assistant on the titles was E. Nelson Bridwell who was a virtual walking encyclopedia of Superman lore. If I came up with what I considered to be an ingenious new innovation or plot twist, I would always run it by Nelson to see if Mort had done something similar with the character during his tenure.

"B.O."

I have always held that one of the cardinal rules is that you must "Be Original" (some even nicknamed me "B. O. Schwartz"), and if Mort had already done it the way I was planning, I would have to come up with new solution. Strangely enough, it was Mort himself who taught me this

lesson. It was back in our fanzine days, and I was writing a
review of a book—or perhaps it was a news article—when I
used an expression like "faster than the speed of light." At
the editing stage (we used to edit each other) Mort came
back to me, laced into me for using the expression, and
told me to change it because he had used it in the
previous issue. As I thought about it I realized that I must
have noticed it and liked it when I read it in his article and
therefore wanted to use it for my own good stead. Mort
wouldn't hear of it. "Be original," he barked. And to this
day, Be Original is my motto . . . just like Mort.

(Thanks, Mort.)

I also needed a new writer whom I could trust to take
over the title, so I turned to the number-one writer in my
stable at the time, Denny O'Neil who had done such great
work on *Batman, Green Lantern*, and *Green Arrow* (as well as
numerous other titles).

Now, like myself, Denny was never a great *Superman* fan
and was not really chomping at the bit to take over the "man
of steel" writing duties for the title . . . but after a bit of coax-
ing, pleading, bargaining, and co-plotting, he agreed to sign
on for a short while.

While I enjoyed working with the talented powerhouses
that were Neal and Denny, I must admit that it was very
tough going.

The best example was when we were working on the
Superman-Muhammad Ali special. It was a major project

for the company, and Jenette Kahn, the publisher, asked me to take care of it.

Denny would write it, I would edit it, and Neal would illustrate it. But when Neal started to adapt it, he started to make changes and didn't follow the script too well.

Denny raised objections until, finally, he said to Neal, "I won't change your artwork if you don't change my copy."

It didn't happen, and Neal kept making changes, and Denny finally quit the project, and Neal had to finish it all by himself, with the final credits as: "Script based on an original Story by Denny O'Neil, Adapted by Neal Adams, and Pencilled by Neal Adams."

The issue's cover was definitely something else! It was a shot of Superman and Ali duking it out in the ring as a huge audience looks on. There are 172 distinct faces in that crowd, ranging from DC characters to Warner employees to celebrities of politics, entertainment, the arts, and sports (including Cher, Donny and Marie, Joe Namath, Jimmy Carter, and Kurt Vonnegut, Jr.). We published a code to all of the faces on the inside cover (yours truly is number eighty-one on the list of celebrities included).

The project kept getting later and later and when the book was published, it came at a disasterous time because Ali had just lost the championship to Leon Spinks.

Now, I don't know if the book didn't do as well as the company had hoped because Ali was no longer champion since in the book he was fighting Superman for championship of the world.

•   •   •

When Alexander (the father) and Ilya (the son) Salkind decided to do the *Superman* movie, they came to DC and talked to me about the project. Ilya asked me who I thought would do a good job on the screenplay.

My first choice was my old friend Leigh Brackett.

Ilya didn't recognize the name and asked who he was, and I had to explain that *she* had scripted numerous John Wayne films as well as *The Big Sleep*, etc., etc., and that she also was a noted science-fiction writer and that her husband, Ed Hamilton, too, was a noted science-fiction author who also knew comics (as well as a former *Superman* writer).

Originally Ilya was interested but quickly dismissed her when he found out that she was in California since he wanted someone who was in the New York area so that they could get down to work right away. (Leigh, as her luck would have it, would soon be busy on a little film called *The Empire Strikes Back* for another enthusiastic filmmaker, by the name of George Lucas.)

I then suggested Alfred Bester and ran down his credits with Ilya, who asked him to do a brief treatment for the movie. Ilya got in touch with Alfie's agent, Lurton Blassingham, and negotiated a deal for more money than Alfie had ever been paid for a single job in his entire life of writing.

An enthusiastic Ilya was quite pleased with himself and reported back to his father, Alexander, and told him that he had signed up a noted SF writer to do the screenplay.

Alexander didn't recognize Alfie's name and scoffed, saying that it wouldn't work out because they needed a top-notch writer for the job. One whose name meant big best-selling success. A celebrated bestseller!

So they wound up paying Alfie a kill fee and signed up Mario Puzo, the bestselling author of *The Godfather*, to do the job. (They were able to pay Puzo as much as they did because they decided to go with an unknown in the part of Superman, a young actor by the name of Christopher Reeve.) As a result, they sent Puzo to meet with me, I briefed him on the character, gave him the comics we were doing, and off he went and wrote the screenplay.

Weeks later, the screenplay was delivered to the Salkinds and they were horrified.

Since when was Clark Kent a television reporter? That simply wouldn't do! (They backed up their opinion with a man-on-the-street poll that asked people to identify who Clark Kent was; almost everyone polled answered: a reporter for the *Daily Planet*. So much for his sojourn as a television reporter.)

The script was changed, and Clark was sent back behind his old newsroom typewriter at the *Daily Planet*. Among the scenes that were dropped from the final screenplay, one dealt with his date with Lois, where he realized that he had neglected to bring any wine for their dinner, and he quickly scanned the world with his telescopic vision for a solution to his problem, saw that the Queen of England was just about to launch a ship with a bottle of champagne, and quickly zoomed across the ocean to England, snatching the bottle out of Her Highness's hands before it smashed against the ship's hull, and delivered it to Lois. The other scene dealt with Lex Luthor, who everyone knows was Supes's bald-headed foe. In the deleted scene, Superman is trying to track down Luthor and homes in on a bald guy in a trench coat, who he grabs and turns around . . . only to find a guy sucking on a lollipop who says to him, "Who loves ya, baby?"—played by, of course, Telly Savalas, whose *Kojak* TV series was very popular at the time. (Unfortunately, Gene Hackman convinced the powers that be that it would be better if he played Luthor with his own hair until the end when he takes it off as if it was really a wig all along to reveal the infamous bald head of Luthor, and as a result, Kojak's cameo was never shot.)

(Another showbiz secret that I was privy to concerned the movie *Supergirl*. As you may recall, the villainess of the movie was an evil witch by the name of Selena who was played by Academy Award-winning actress Faye Dunaway . . . but she was not the first choice for the role. The producers offered their first choice a lot of money but she turned them down because she didn't want to play a villain, not even one that was played for laughs. Their first choice for the part was the bountiful and buxom Dolly Parton.)

After a while I was looked on by my bosses at DC as a sort of media good-luck charm. After all I had taken over *Batman* and —*POW!*— a hit TV series. Then I took over *Superman* and —*BAM!*— a hit movie. So then I was asked to take over a series called *Dial H for Hero* in hopes of getting a series off the ground. I took over and *THUD!*

Well, not even Babe Ruth hit a homer every time at bat.

Accepting the honorary Nebula Award for Siegel and Shuster in 1979 from Jack Williamson, president of the Science Fiction Writers of America.

• • •

In the late seventies, when Jack Williamson (who was an old friend of Jerry Siegel) was serving a term as president of the Science Fiction Writers of America (from 1978 to 1979), he arranged for a special honorary Nebula Award to be given to Siegel and Shuster as "the originators of *Superman* for creating an American myth." Since they were unable to attend, I accepted for them.

OTHER EARLY INFLUENCES ON THE CREATION OF SUPERMAN

Clark Kent's appearance and career were based on Walter Dennis, a Chicago newspaper reporter and science-fiction fan with whom Jerry Siegel corresponded in 1930,

The real Clark Kent: newspaperman Walter Dennis.

and his name was derived from a combination of two actors' names—"Clark" from Clark Gable, who was the most popular actor of the time, and "Kent" from Kent Taylor, who though obviously not as popular as Gable did happen to be Jerry's wife's relative.

Jerry's wife-to-be Joanne, was the model for the original Lois Lane.

Planet Krypton derived its name from the same source that Edgar Rice Burroughs used in his Barsoon Mars novels. The capital of Barsoon was Helium, so Siegel decided to call Superman's home Krypton from the same Table of Periodic Elements.

In addition to being a fan of Burroughs, Jerry Siegel also really enjoyed the Doc Savage pulp stories by Lester Dent and incorporated several other elements into his development of Superman's identity. Doc had a secret headquarters that was fortified; Superman got a Fortress of Solitude. Doc was known as "the Man of Bronze"; Superman, "the Man of Steel."

Jack Williamson once told me that early in his career he had written and published a story called "The Girl from Mars," which dealt with a nuclear explosion that was about to occur on the planet Mars (shades of the destruction of Krypton) and a Martian scientist who managed to send his infant daughter to safety on nearby planet Earth, where she could be safely brought up (a plot line exceptionally similar to baby Kal-El's escape).

Finally, the name of Superman's father, Jor-El, is in reality a partial anagram taken from Jerome Siegel (the name that Jerry Siegel used in his early Superman stories), thus he is the father of Superman both as creator and anagramatically.

For the 400th issue of *Superman* we decided to put out a sixty-four page anniversary issue that included a dozen or so pinups of the Man of Steel done by artists who had never worked on Superman previously. People like Walt Simonson, John Byrne (who would later take over the series), Mike Grell, Moebius (who did his sketch on his flight from Paris to New York), Bernie Wrightson, Steve Ditko, Frank Miller, Will Eisner, Jack Kirby, and even Milton Caniff of *Terry and the Pirates* and *Steve Canyon* fame were all invited to take part.

This turned out to be the only time I ever got to work

with either Will Eisner, the creator of *The Spirit*, or with the legendary Jack Kirby (I remember having to introduce Jack at an Atlanta Fantasy Fair one year even though we had never really worked together besides on that one pinup, and as a result I introduced him by saying, "Joe Shuster and Jerry Siegel created *Superman*, Bob Kane and Bill Finger created *Batman*, and Jack Kirby created everything else"—which, when you get right down to it, isn't really that of much of an exaggeration.

Milton Caniff did a real nice piece that we had to unfortunately drop from the issue. It depicted Superman leaving a phone booth having just changed into his costume as Steve Canyon watched from a distance. It was a great pinup, but unfortunately the rights to the character of Steve Canyon were controlled by a newspaper syndicate, and things would have taken way too long to get permission to use the character in our comic, given our deadline, so in the end we had to run the issue without it.

One of the odd things that Caniff's piece pointed out was the importance of the phone booth in the Superman mythos—and the funny thing is that, like kryptonite, it didn't originate in the comics but was later incorporated into them despite the idea's silliness since phone booths didn't really obscure enough if anyone wanted to use one as a changing room for switching costumes. (There is a great nod to this motif in the first *Superman* film where Christopher Reeve is getting ready to go into action as the Man of Steel and is looking for a place to change out of his Clark Kent duds. His first inclination is to seek out a phone booth, but unfortunately the phone booths of 1970s were no longer really booths but sort of half shells without even doors on them. There is a wonderfully panicked look on Reeve's face when he realizes this and moves on in search of another place (which turns out to be a revolving door that he manipulates with super speed so that no one will see him. It was just another very neat inside joke that Superman fans could really appreciate.)

Superman #400 included a script by Elliot Maggin that was illustrated by one of the most distinguished illustrator lineups in comic book history! It included pages by Joe Orlando, Marshall Rogers, Klaus Janson, Frank Miller, Wendy Pini, Mike Kaluta, Al Williamson, and Jim Steranko—all artists who had never drawn Superman before. The overall story was titled "The Living Legends of Superman."

In 1985 I turned seventy, and all of my friends and co-workers at DC were not about to let it pass without making a fuss. I kind of knew this but not to the extent of the stunt that they were able to pull off.

Elliot Maggin, one of my writers, approached executive vice president Paul Levitz with the idea of doing a special Julie Schwartz issue of *Superman* that would feature me as a character (thus giving DC the opportunity to copyright and trademark me, I guess). The idea was to do the entire issue behind my back, so it could be my birthday surprise . . . and they sure pulled it off.

Elliot and Curt Swan secretly worked behind my back in

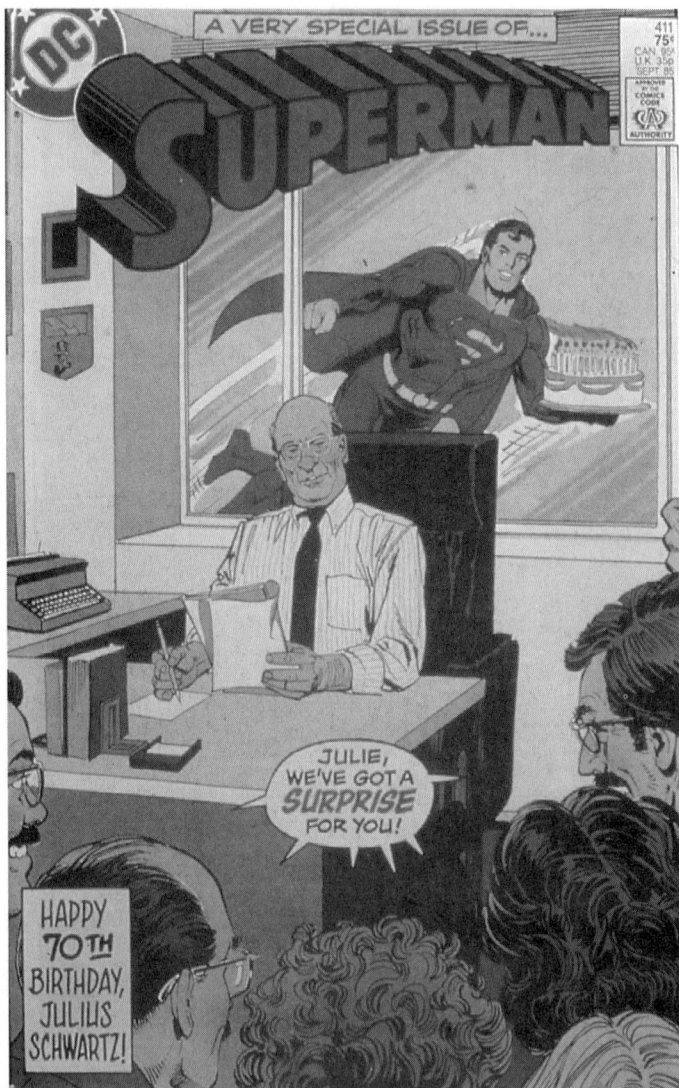

Superman #411. Only the Man of Steel could lift a cake with 70 candles. (©2000 DC Comics)

close collaboration with Bob Rozakis in the production department to complete the entire issue so that it could be inserted in the schedule and would come out at the appropriate time in place of the issue I had been working on, which would be delayed a month.

So comes the day, and all of a sudden publisher Jenette Kahn's administrative assistant Carol Fein comes in and says we're having a special meeting in the conference room. I probably fretted as I walked down the hall wondering what the latest crisis was—and walked into the conference room to discover champagne on ice and Jenette handing me the first copy of *Superman* #411, and I see that I am depicted on the cover.

My first thoughts were *My God! How could you do this to me? I was right in the middle of a three-part story about Luthor*— and I repeated my thoughts out loud.

Everyone laughed, and then so did I.

I looked more closely at the issue. I wasn't just featured on the cover. The entire issue was about me and my career and some of the people I have known and what it might have been like had I lived in a parallel universe where Superman really existed.

The festivities then continued with reading of well wishes from my friends, telephone greetings from Ray Bradbury (who was also a character in the story) and Alan Moore, and a long telegram greeting from Harlan Ellison.

Certainly it must rank as was one of the major highlights of my fifty-plus-year career in comics.

ASIMOV'S SUPERMAN STORY

I once asked Isaac Asimov, whom I had known early in my days of fandom as just another pushy, snot-nosed kid from Brooklyn (way before he became one of the most lauded SF writers of all time), if he would do a story for me at DC, perhaps a Superman story.

Isaac thought about it for a a while and made a pitch :

> The world is at peace, and the devil comes to claim Superman's soul, having fulfilled all of his wishes and enabled him to accomplish everything he wanted. The story would then be Supes going to hell and trying to get out of it.

He never got around to doing it, so I was never able to find out how he was going to make it all work out (he balked at actually doing the story when he realized how little he really knew about Superman).

I often wonder how things might have been different had I agreed to represent him at the same time that I succumbed to Bradbury's pleadings. Isaac was at the convention, and we had met before . . . but he was much too pushy and too much of a know-it-all at the time.

Oh, well.

When I gave up editorship of *Superman* after over six hundred Superman-related stories, I decided that I had to have him go out with a bang, and I also decided to approach it as if the entire series was going to come to an end and that all of the loose plot threads needed to be resolved. Did

Superman ever marry Lois? Did he die? What about the Justice League? What happened to the villains—Luthor, Toyman, Brainiac, etc.? How about his friends Jimmy Olsen, Perry White, and Lana Lang? All of these questions would have to be resolved.

For my swan song with the Supes, I knew that the choice of writer was of the utmost importance . . . but who would that be?

Really, there was only one choice: the original creator, Jerry Siegel, the man who had started it all way back when.

So I called up Jerry, and we arranged to meet at the San Diego Comic Con to discuss the project. I offered him the job, and he was thrilled despite the fact that he would no doubt have to do a lot of homework on what the Man of Steel had been up to in recent years. He immediately accepted.

Then we hit a stumbling block.

Jerry would have to sign a work-for-hire contract in order to get paid, and this was something that he had promised his brother-in-law (who was a lawyer) he would never do again having lost all rights to the Superman characters all those years ago when he signed a work-for-hire agreement for the first Superman story in *Action Comics* back in 1938.

This was a problem!

Jerry decided that it·was too good a job to pass up, so he offered to do it *sans* contract—which unfortunately would never fly for DC, so in the end he had to bow out entirely.

The next morning, I couldn't stop thinking about finding a replacement for Jerry. I was having breakfast with a young writer by the name of Alan Moore, with whom I had a good working relationship, and mentioned my predicament to him in hopes of blue skying some possible solutions.

At that point he literally leaped out of his chair, reached across the table, put his hands around my neck, and said, "If you let anybody but me write that story, I'll kill you!" And since I didn't want to be an accessory to my own murder, I agreed.

In a letter dated 9/19/85, I wrote to Alan:

> The time has come! Meaning that I've just been informed that the September cover dated issues of *Superman* and *Action* will be my last . . .
>
> What I'm getting at is: The time has come for you to type up the story your "mouth" agreed to do—that is, an imaginary Superman that would serve as the last Superman story if the magazines were discontinued—what would happen to Superman, Clark Kent, Lois Lane, Lana Lang, Jimmy Olsen, Perry White, Luthor, Brainiac, Mr. Mxyzptik, and all of the et cetera you can deal with.

. . . and by God he did just that with a story entitled "Whatever Happened to the Man of Tomorrow?" which is considered by many (including me!) to be the finest Superman story ever written.

Curt Swan was chosen to be the artist because many considered him to be the signature artist on the series for the past thirty years. The *Superman* issue was then inked by George Perez, while the *Action* issue was inked by Kurt

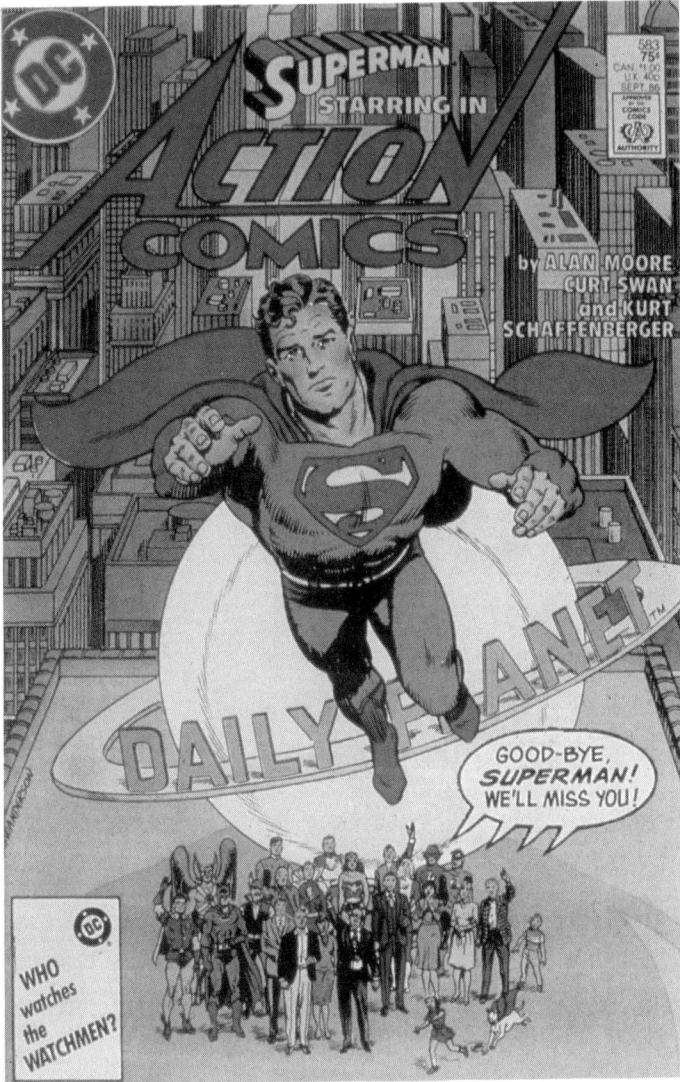

Artist Curt Swan had Superman shedding a few tears for our last issue, Action Comics #583. (©2000 DC Comics)

Schaffenberger, and the covers were done by legendary Swan collaborator Murphy Anderson, thus giving the so-called Swanderson team once last chance to shine on this series.

It was the perfect way to finish out my run on the title. In the legend that precedes the story, Alan Moore wrote the truest thing ever said about comics: "This is an imaginary story. . . . Aren't they all?"

On the cover of the last issue, which featured the second part of the story (in *Action*), Superman is flying off with his superhero friends, waving good-bye. In the forefront are a few nonsuperheroes: a young woman based on DC publisher and president Jenette Kahn; on one side of her is a man based on Curt Swan, the artist who did the last years of my tenure on the title; and on the other side is a balding, bespectacled fellow who bears more than a passing resemblance to yours truly.

After I left the custodianship of *Superman*, the series was turned over to John Byrne (formally of Marvel Comics fame) who reinvented a lot of the mythos in "the Man of Steel" series. We were all at an affair at the Smithsonian Institution celebrating *Superman's* anniversary when I spied Curt Swan and John Byrne in the same room together. Thinking quickly, I handed Curt a pen and suggested that he hand it over to John, which he did.

It was the perfect photo opportunity to symbolize the passing of an era as one artist turned the pen over to another artist, who would succeed him in his duties.

PART FIVE

LIFE AFTER BATMAN AND SUPERMAN AND OTHER CONVENTION-AL ADVENTURES

■ ver the years of my tenure on *Batman* and on *Superman*, numerous changes had occurred in the DC Comics hierarchy. Carmine Infantino had been succeeded as president by Sol Harrison and then by a lovely and vivacious red-headed beauty by the name of Jenette Kahn.

Jenette had been new to the pantheon of DC characters and the way comic books were put together, but she had been willing to learn. Occasionally, maybe when I was working on an idea for a story with say Cary Bates or someone, she would just come into the office and just sit off to the side and just listen to how we were doing it . . . sort of like a school principal doing an evaluation on a teacher; more so like a person who actually wanted to get a better idea of how the people under her really worked. It was as much an education for her as it was for us.

Jenette was always very good to me and my family. On one occasion, she took us to a Yankees game and a dinner. It was the day that Billy Martin was rehired (for the umpteenth time) by George Steinbrenner. The Yanks lost that day.

And of course she did the OKing for my seventy-fifth birthday festivities.

THE THREE THINGS I LEARNED AT CITY COLLEGE OF NEW YORK

1) "Elephants" are better to say for counting seconds than "Mississippis."
2) Stalactites hang from the ceiling (C for ceiling) and stalagmites come up from the ground (G for ground).
3) VIBGYOR—which stands for "violet, indigo, blue, green, yellow, orange, and red," the colors of the spectrum—is a handy thing to know if you're working in comic books. (It's also known as ROY G. BIV.)

In addition to new faces it was also a thrill to see old faces working their way up through the ranks, like such artists as Joe Orlando and Dick Giordano and writers like Denny O'Neil.

Back in the seventies, DC had a bunch of young eager beavers hanging around the office. They were fans mostly, with names like Len Wein, Marv Wolfman, Paul Kupperberg, Martin Pasko, and Paul Levitz, all of whom hoped to break into the business of funny books.

One of these dedicated fans, Paul Levitz, was a student at Stuyvesant High School (where he studied under Frank McCourt, who twenty years later would become the best-selling Pulitzer Prize–winning author of *Angela's Ashes*). Paul worked as an assistant to Joe Orlando in his spare time. Part gofer, part record keeper, part copy editor, basically whatever Joe wanted him to do. Paul eventually became a quite talented scripter, but the way he broke into the writing side of the business was more bizarre than any story ever published by DC.

Bill Finger (who as I mentioned earlier was the best scripter in the business and the true cocreator of Batman) late in his career had become a bit unreliable when it came to delivery dates. The work would be fine, and he would get it done—just sometimes a week or two later than when you really needed it. So one day Bill comes in to deliver some work to Joe, who instructs Paul to handle it. It was a Friday, and following in the footsteps of the ever reliable Schwartz, a check had already been cut so that Bill could be paid right on the day of delivery. There was only one problem, though:

Bill was supposed to be delivering two scripts, and he had only one finished, but he gave his word to Paul that he would have the other one in on Monday. Paul, still partially in awe at the idea of working with one of the greatest living comic-book legends, believed him and gave him the check for the two jobs, figuring that Bill was good for his word . . . and Bill probably would have been had he not died that weekend.

The following Monday, therefore, Paul had a problem. He had paid Bill for a script that he had not delivered (which was against policy and probably even against his own better judgment), and Joe was still waiting for the undelivered work, which was by now way over deadline. Only one solution was available to the resourceful lad. He knew he was going to have to tell Joe what happened but didn't want to compound the problem by coming in empty-handed, so he asked permission to make it up by writing a substitute script, figuring that he could only be fired once—and whether it was for a bad script or just a dumb mistake, it really didn't matter much.

Joe agreed, and Paul kept his job.

Paul, of course, wanted to continue as a scripter and soon tried his hand at a feature length story for *Adventure*. Carmine saw all books at cover conference stage in those days, and seeing Paul's young writer byline, decided to pass it to me for my opinion. So he brought it into my office and asked me to give it a quick look (as Joe had to admit that he liked the kid and might be biased in his own judgment). I read it carefully and shared my verdict. The script was fine, no real problems, even though it was a bit more of the Marvel school than the DC school of storytelling. It even showed some potential for first-class scripting, raw talent that might one day be polished to the level of a Bill Finger or John Broome. I told Carmine my thoughts.

Paul's script went in, and more feature-length assignments followed.

Today Paul is executive vice-president and publisher of DC Comics, the number-two person in the entire organization—and to think, little did I know at that moment in the seventies, I once literally held the future of his entire career in the palm of my hand.

JULIE'S HINTS ON WORKING IN COMICS DURING THE SILVER AGE PART ONE: THE THREE WORDS YOU MUST NEVER USE

When I first started off in comics, a wise man named Shelly Mayer gave me some advice, which I will now impart to you.

If you don't want to get in trouble:

1. Never call a character CLINT
2. Never use the verb FLICK
3. And always avoid using the contraction WHO'RE

A slip up in the lettering can end your career faster than Clint can flick his Bic.

After I left the editorship of *Superman*, I handled various different projects for DC.

One of the ones that I was most enthusiastic about was a series of science-fiction graphic novels. When DC said that they were going ahead with a graphic-novel series, I injected myself into the process and explained that I wasn't too happy with their previous attempts in the field. I thought that it would be better to take some classic science-fiction stories by recognizable SF authors. Instead of doing them as simply a glossy comic book, go all out and produce them as differently as possible so that they would stand out as something really unique on the rack.

Now, when I said "classic," I didn't mean as in H. G. Wells and Jules Verne or similar outdated stories I'd read during my boyhood (back when dinosaurs roamed the earth) but rather award-winning stories by some of contemporary top science-fiction writers. I figured that if they had won Hugos or Nebula Awards, they had to have been pretty good to start with, and that prestige would have a certain amount of promotional value for our new venture.

Roughly around this time I was a guest at the 1984 World Science Fiction Convention in Anaheim, where I reacquainted myself with old friends whom I hadn't seen for years since previously my job at DC didn't bring me into contact with the SF community from whence I had originally come. As the stalwarts of my past like Hamilton, Kuttner, and Binder were no longer around, I took this opportunity to scout some appropriate stories for the new SF graphic-novel line.

The first person I contacted was Robert Bloch (whose last foray into comics was, as I mentioned before, less than

MAN OF TWO WORLDS

memorable for him). He remembered a story of his that I
had acted as an agent on entitled "Hell On Earth," and since
it had not appeared in any collected anthology, he suggested
that we give that one a try.

So he sent me a copy of the story, and we cleared the
rights and did it as the first book in the series, illustrated by
Keith Giffen and inked and colored by Greg Theakston.

(Although we called the series science fiction, we didn't
restrict our chooses to pure SF and wanted to include fantasy, some mystery, horror, and hopefully eventually something by a very popular young writer by the name of
Stephen King.)

Part of the 1986 WorldCon package included a free pass
to Disneyland, and after a ten-hour day in the park I was
exhausted and was leaning against the wall when I saw
another exhausted wall-leaner I thought I recognized as
being part of the convention. Len Wein told me that it was
Robert Silverberg, so I decided to go over and introduce
myself.

"Excuse me, Mr. Silverberg," I said, "you don't know me
but my name is Julie Schwartz."

"Julie Schwartz!" he exclaimed. "Harlan Ellison told me
all about you. You are a living legend. What can I do for
you?"

I explained that I was waiting for some friends who were
souvenir shopping, and he admitted that the young lady that
he was there with was doing the same and suggested that we
ditch our parties and go back to the hotel for a drink.

I agreed.

Along the way I mentioned that I was editing a series of graphic novels that would be illustrated editions of outstanding SF stories and did he have any in mind that we would be appropriate. He thought about it and suggested his award-winning story *Nightwings*.

I said great and asked him who his agent was.

He said he was repped by Kirby McCauley but I could deal with him directly thus saving him paying Kirby fifteen percent of a deal that he had nothing to do with.

I was paying fifteen hundred dollars for the rights of the stories in the series, and that was fine with him, and we shook on it.

A few weeks later Silverberg called and asked where his check for the fifteen hundred dollars was. I asked him if he had given DC his social security number and all of the pertinent information, and he admitted that he hadn't as of yet. So I jotted it down and told him that I would expedite his check. Before getting off the phone, I felt compelled to ask him a question.

"Bob, what's the hurry?" I asked. "I just read in *Locus* that you just signed a big-money deal for a few books. Why are you worried about a mere fifteen hundred dollars?"

"Oh, well, that's just money-to-come for cash in the bank. This is walking-around money."

(Bob and I became good friends, and I learned that he was a great fan of Henry Kuttner and C. L. Moore, so I offered him the choice of a book signed by Kuttner or one by Moore from my private collection of their works. He promised to treasure it for the rest of his life. (Kutter inscribed several of the books to me personally; my favorite was inscribed by Kuttner to me with the inscription TO JULIE SCHWARTZ BECAUSE HIS HEART IS PURE.)

The story was handed over to Cary Bates, who did a fine script with pencil work by Gene Colan over which an extraordinary paint job was done by Neal McPheeters.

The third story I lined up was from Ray Bradbury, who, though he didn't attend the convention, made time for me in his busy schedule when he came to New York. Obviously his novels would have been a problem for the project. Most of them were too long and involved for our purposes, and, besides, they had already been adapted for television, the movies, or the stage, or they were optioned for such adaptation in the future. I asked him about some of his shorter stories and if any of them might suit the series.

Ray knew of one immediately and said, "Yes, as a matter of fact you sold it for me many years ago. It was called 'The Eight Day Planet,' and it dealt with an alien world where the average lifespan of birth to death of old age was under eight days." I knew the story and thought it would be perfect. It was retitled as "Frost and Fire," and Klaus Janson (of *Batman: The Dark Knight Returns* fame) adapted the entire work on it—scripting, pencils, inks, and coloring.

Frederik Pohl was my next target, and he recommended his story "The Merchants of Venus," which introduced and serves as prequel to his award-winning and bestselling Heechee saga.

Larry Niven then contributed "The Magic Goes Away" and George R. R. Martin (who has never forgiven me for not publishing any of his letters to me in any of the letter columns I edited during my tenure back in the sixties and seventies) offered his award-winning masterpiece *Sand Kings* (which was later adapted for Showtime's *Outer Limits* TV series).

Speaking of *Outer Limits*, perhaps the real find that we added to the list was a previously uncollected work by Harlan Ellison. It was entitled "Demon with a Glass Hand" and was a teleplay of an episode from the original *Outer Limits* television show of the sixties, featuring an early performance by Robert Culp in his pre-*I Spy* days. We worked directly from Harlan's teleplay (no rescripting or adapting) and the artwork was done by Marshall Rogers.

No one could criticize the quality of the stories, the scripts, or the artwork in the graphic novels we were doing, but unfortunately the series never took off. In retrospect, maybe we should have led off with the lure of an Asimov or a Clarke or a Heinlein or even a King to attract more attention to the series. Unfortunately our different format was not really comic-shop friendly (it was oversized and almost squareish) and at that time the book trade shied away from graphic novels, thus limiting our distribution.

It was a bold experiment and a good effort, but it didn't work, and, much to my disappointment, the series folded.

Another post-*Superman* project I was involved with concerned a spinoff series featuring one of the villains that had been introduced during my last months as *Superman*'s editor. The character was called "the Ambush Bug," who was supposedly a native of that alien place called New Jersey and was developed by a talented though wacky and way-out fellow by the name of Keith Giffen (who, as I mentioned previously, adapted Bob Bloch's story in the graphic-novel series). Strictly speaking, I was less than an editor on the title and in fact became a character in the series itself as the "supervillain" series metamorphasized into a satire on the entire comic book industry and corporate America.

At one point the Ambush Bug seeks out the cushiest job in the world and decides to take over my job at DC since I never do any real work, am loved all by one and all, etc., etc. So he takes a trip in a time machine to the far future to find out when I would be retiring only to discover that I am still employed by DC even though I am now only a disembodied head.

It's quite an odd feeling to see a head with your own likeness bouncing from comic book panel to comic book panel, and the short-lived *Ambush Bug* series was probably the wackiest product of my editorial career that I ever worked on.

My return to the science-fiction convention scene (which I partially owe to Los Angeles Science Fiction Society fan Craig Miller, who invited me to the Anaheim World Science Fiction Convention to receive the prestigious Forry Award) turned out to be quite an agreeable thing for everyone involved. I liked seeing old friends, and DC especially enjoyed having me as their sort of goodwill ambassador to the convention scene. They even printed up flyers announcing my availability in the form of a WANTED poster which read:

WANTED

by comic and science fiction fans for Convention Appearances

JULIUS SCHWARTZ

A.K.A. the only living legend in both comics and science fiction

Description: NOTORIOUS DC COMICS EDITOR

Known hits: The FLASH—20 years

BATMAN—16 years

SUPERMAN—16 years

STRANGE ADVENTURES—13 years

(in fact, for forty plus years no genre of DC Comics has been considered safe)

WARNING! If you are interested in having Julie appear at your upcoming convention, we urge you to notify: [etc., etc.]

I was a multitrack guest for most conventions and had slide shows prepared for Golden Age science fiction, the origins of science-fiction fandom, the Silver Age of comics, and, of course, one devoted to the big guy in the red-and-blue tights. I was amazed to find out that so many people knew who I was. Not just regular Joes like myself but real celebrities like Mark Hamill (aka Luke Skywalker), Caroline Munro (star of numerous Ray Harryhausen and Hammer Studios productions), and David Prowse (aka Darth Vader). At one point there was a band that occasionally played the San Diego Comic Con and a few other conventions. Its name was "Seduction of the Innocent" (a sarcastic tip of the

Fellow living legends and fannish friends. On couch, from left: Jack Kirby, Jerry Siegel, Bob Kane, and Miguel Ferrer. Behind them: Bill Mumy. Foreground: Mark Hamill. (Ilene Mumy)

hat to the propaganda book from the fifties that declared that comic books were bad for you) and among its members were Bill Mumy (of *Lost in Space* and *Babylon 5*), Max Allan Collins (award-winning mystery novel writer as well as a pretty darn good comic scripter), and Miguel Ferrer (son of José and star in his own right of *Twin Peaks* and *Lateline*) . . . and they all took time out of their busy schedules to hang out with me.

I took my position as comics' elder statesman quite seriously, particularly on the convention circuit. It was easy not to bad mouth anyone or cause trouble because I kept most of my opinions to myself—and quite frankly, unless I was currently assigned to a given title, I didn't read it. Therefore, if someone wanted to know what I thought of John Byrne's take on Superman, or the latest version of Green Lantern, I would tell the truth and say I didn't know because I hadn't read them.

There were a few things that I did have opinions on, however.

When I went to the Dallas Fantasy Fair they used to ask me if I would help to present the Jack Kirby Hall of Fame Award. I inquired as to how many were being inducted and was shocked to find that it was only one person—just ONE! (That year was to be Wally Wood, who had recently passed away.) Wally had done inking on some Gil Kane pencils for me once, and I knew his ex-wife so I agreed to accept the award and present it to her.

The next year the Jack Kirby Hall of Fame Award was to go to Alex Toth, and I agreed to accept it for him, but warned them that it would be the last time that I would take part in the ceremony unless there was more than one winner—and moreover if they wanted me to take part in next year's ceremony, I would demand to have some influence over who was going to get the award. When asked who I had in mind, I shot back "Jerry Siegel and Joe Shuster, who should have been the first recipients!" . . . and . . . the year after, the choice had to be Bob Kane and Bill Finger. In my mind it was unthinkable that we could be honoring people and inducting them into a comics hall of fame without ever giving the award to the creators of *Superman* and *Batman*.

On another occasion the featured speaker was R. Crumb, the creator of Fritz the Cat and other classic alternative comic-book characters, and Crumb at the last minute decided to beg off on delivering his keynote speech, so it fell to me to sub for him. Now, unaccustomed as I am to public speaking, I accepted the assignment and spent most of the time talking about Joe Shuster, who was in poor health at that time, and the Superman legacy, which is obviously quite a deviation from the antiestablishment concerns of Crumb.

(After the Dallas conventions closed down, the awards were moved to Oakland's WonderCon.)

There also were the Will Eisner Hall of Fame Awards that were given out at the San Diego Comic Con, and for many years I was hoping that I would eventually receive one; though I had been nominated several times, alas I had never received one.

In 1997, I was suffering from a particularly bad case of arthritis and sciatica, and had decided that I would have to forego the convention and the awards ceremony. When my decision was made known to the convention, I received a call from comics maven Mark Evanier, who informed me that I was slated to receive the Will Eisner Hall of Fame Award that year and that if I couldn't make it, who did I want to accept the award for me.

I thought for a minute and decided that I would ask Gil Kane to do the honors (Gil did not usually like to attend award ceremonies but I knew that he would do this as a favor to me).

Mark was pleased when he heard my choice because he confided in me that Gil was also going to receive the award. So when the night of the awards came around, and the master of ceremonies, Sergio Aragonés, announced my name, Gil went to the stage and accepted the award on my behalf. He was about to return to his seat when he was told to stick around for a moment, at which point they presented him with a Will Eisner Hall of Fame Award, completely surprising him.

JULIE'S HINTS ON WORKING IN COMICS
DURING THE SILVER AGE
PART TWO:
THE SECRET OF SUCCESSFUL
COMIC BOOK COVERS

Contrary to popular belief, during my early days of comics, the schedule would sometimes dictate that we design the cover before the story that it illustrated had even been conceived of yet.

Experience eventually yielded a few secrets that helped us to predict what would be a successful cover.

Show the planet Earth in Danger

We depicted the Earth being towed away by a gigantic spaceship. We showed the Earth being cut in half by a gigantic saw. I showed a cover in which there were two Earths in space. The copy in the word balloon said to a space traveler who was returning to Earth: IF YOU LAND ON THE REAL EARTH, THE EARTH WILL BE SPARED. BUT IF YOU LAND ON THE COUNTERFEIT EARTH, THE REAL EARTH WILL BE BLOWN UP. And he had to figure out which one was which.

Show duplicate superheroes

A superhero with a duplicate of himself—be it Flash or Green Lantern or whomever—always sold well.

Show superheroes fighting each other or in competition

A fight breaks out, and everyone is hooked (even if it later turns out that the fight was just a setup). Readers loved to see their favorite heroes in conflict.

Competitions were good, too. Who was faster, Flash or Superman? Those race covers always sold well.

We even once pitted Superman against Muhammad Ali. That was indeed the fight of the century!

Command the reader

One of my favorites is a cover for the <u>Flash</u>. All it showed was a stark closeup of the Flash holding up his hand toward the reader as if he was a traffic cop. The balloon read, STOP! DON'T PASS UP THIS ISSUE! MY LIFE DEPENDS ON IT!

Who could resist buying that issue and saving the scarlet speedster's life?

From that basic idea we worked out the story, and it sold very well.

A Gorilla on the cover doing something un-gorillalike will surely sell!

I edited a comic called <u>Strange Adventures</u>, which normally sold pretty well, and then one day the editorial director came in and asked "What happened to <u>Strange Adventures</u>?"

"Why?" I inquired.

One of my all-time favorite covers: Flash #163. (©2000 DC
Comics)

"Why? Because it had a tremendous sale, that's why!"

So we decided to look at the cover for a clue to its success.

The cover was roughly a scene like this:

It was set in a zoo and we are looking at a group of people looking at a gorilla in a cage. Among the crowd was a pretty girl. Now the gorilla had a slate in his hand and a piece of chalk, and he'd written out the following message on the slate: RUTH . . . PLEASE BELIEVE ME! I AM THE VICTIM OF A TERRIBLE SCIENTIFIC EXPERIMENT!—RALPH.

Well, it must have been that this idea—a gorilla who was once a man, pleading with his girlfriend to help him out of this horrendous situation—appealed to our readers. They wanted to know how such a thing could possibly happen and what could be done about it.

We decided that the magazine sold well because the gorilla was acting like a human being. So we decided to try it again . . . and every time we tried it, it sold fantastically well, with sales shooting sky high!

In due time every editor wanted to use a gorilla on the cover. Even on <u>Wonder Woman</u>! Eventually the law had to be laid down: no more than one DC cover that had a gorilla on it a month (except, of course for the occasional "gorilla month," where every title had to have a gorilla on its cover).

The West Coast conventions always gave me the chance to look in on old friends from both of my previous careers.

Bob Kane used to have a table at Mirabelle's restaurant in Los Angeles (if he called in advance it would be reserved for him without question—even management called it Bob Kane's table), and when I was passing through—usually in connection with the San Diego Comic Con—I would try to schedule a dinner with him at his preferred haunt.

On one particular occasion I told him I would be bringing a friend of mine if he didn't object. He asked me who it was, and I told him it was Ray Bradbury. Bob said fine and met us at the restaurant.

Somehow word got around the restaurant that Ray Bradbury was dining there and before you could say *Fahrenheit 451* everyone was abuzz. Now, Bob was used to being fawned over at "his" restaurant. The first Tim Burton *Batman* movie was in the theaters, and usually an evening didn't go by when he was dining at his table that someone didn't send over a request for the autograph of the man who created Batman. So he became a little miffed at the attention that was being paid to one of his dinner companions rather than himself (one of the waiters actually rushed over to a nearby bookstore to pick up a copy of *The Martian Chronicles* for Ray to inscribe).

The next year rolled around, and I was once again on my way home from San Diego, and I called Bob to set up our usual dinner and mentioned that I would be bringing a guest along.

Bob became guarded and said, "It's not Ray Bradbury is it?"

I assured him it wasn't, and he said fine.

The friend I brought along was Harlan Ellison, who,

though he didn't distract the crowds from Bob, did manage to bend Bob's ear throughout the entire meal. Bob seemed to enjoy the adulation, but afterward he complained that he was hard of hearing in that ear from the workout that Harlan gave it that night.

Another time Bob came down to San Diego to be the Con's guest of honor and to promote his autobiography, *Batman and Me*. Bob was doing a signing, and I noticed Frank Miller walking by and asked him if he would like to meet Bob (Frank was quite a comics celebrity at the time, having just finished the graphic novel *Batman: The Dark Knight Returns*). Frank said sure, and I brought him over and introduced them.

The two shook hands and chatted for a bit until Frank got called away for some other bit of business. When Frank left, Bob took me aside and said, "That Frank Miller! Do you know what he did to Batman? He made him look like Quasimodo the bell-ringing hunchback of Notre Dame!" And to a certain extent Bob was right—but the fans didn't seem to mind.

Later that day, Will Eisner was doing another signing, and I grabbed Bob and snuck him onto the autograph line (Bob and Will and had attended high school together and had been close friends but had drifted apart over the years). When Bob got to the head of the line, Will looked up, did a double take and then a triple take and leaped to his feet to embrace Bob. They later made a date for drinks and renewed old acquaintances.

•   •   •

Probably my two best West Coast friends are Ray Bradbury and Harlan Ellison. Though I have gone on about my role in Ray's early careers, I haven't really said enough about my pal Harlan.

Mr. Harlan Ellison claims that I am the one who was responsible for launching his writing career.

Yes, I guess, I am the one to blame/honor for one of the most talented writers of the twentieth century.

As Harlan tells it, he sent me a letter back in the '40s, and I wrote back to him (note: I was credited with inserting full addresses in the letters-to-the-editors columns in comic books to maximize and encourage fan input and communication). He also claims that he saw me in my office at DC Comics in the late '40s but was stricken silent with awe (note: a silent Harlan Ellison is not likely). A year later he wrote asking me for a piece of *Hawkman* art for his son and I wrote him back. (Harlan later confesses he had no son . . . but did have a stepson at the time of his letter!)

About 1946 or 1947 a letter came into DC Comics where I was an editor from a young fan and a lover of comics, and in this letter he said that he loved DC Comics so much that he hoped to one day become a writer. The young correspondent went on to say that he had checked all of his spelling and grammar and then asked me as editor if I thought that he had any chance of becoming a writer. I wrote him back an encouraging note that basically said that if he really wanted to and worked hard at it, he could become a professional writer.

That youngster started to write, and in 1947 he had a letter printed in *Real Fact Comics* and the letter said that his parents welcomed *Real Fact Comics* as wholeheartedly as he did (it was eleven words long) . . . and that was the literary debut of Harlan Ellison.

In 1971, Harlan offered to write me a *Batman* story, and I said great! He made my day!

And then the waiting started. Days turned into years!

Finally in 1981, ten years later, there I was at the San Diego Comic Con to accept an Inkpot Award from Ray Bradbury, and I was about to leave the stage when Harlan bounced onto the stage springing out of nowhere, a sheaf of pages in hand and announced, "Here it is, the Batman story I promised Julie ten years ago!"

The crowd went wild with applause, so no one heard him when he whispered to me up close that he only had time to do the first page so all the rest of the script was still blank.

Five years later the final script came in, and it was worth the wait.

Harlan also got me interviewed for *Sci-Fi Buzz* on the Sci-Fi channel, and he wished me a happy eighty-third birthday on nationwide television while he was being interviewed on Tom Snyder's late-night talk show.

Harlan has gotten a bad rep from many people who have grown to fear him based on apocryphal exploits (Isaac Asimov, another very close friend of Harlan's, did once state that "'Tis is better to be a friend of Harlan Ellison than an enemy") . . . but the key to all of these legends is that Harlan demands no less a degree of perfection and fairness in others than he is willing to live up to himself.

Ray Bradbury, Harlan Ellison, and me at the 1981 Inkpot Awards in San Diego. (Jackie Estrada)

What many people may not be aware of are the great acts of charity Harlan performs on a regular basis.

At the 1986 WorldCon in Atlanta, Georgia (that was the first time I met a very pretty girl by the name of Jean Dillard, who went on to write a few *Star Trek* novels and a horror novel for the *Abyss* line), that Harlan had come to the Con solely for the purpose of holding and running the benefit auction for Frances Wellman, the widow of Manly Wade Wellman, who had recently died, to help pay for the huge amount of medical bills that were still left.

It was right around this time that DC had done a special issue of *Superman* (#411) with myself as a character, and I had a few copies on hand for the convention and got one autographed by Jerry Siegel and his wife (the model for the original Lois Lane), added my own signature to the mix, and gave it to Harlan for the auction. I think it fetched a little over two hundred dollars, which isn't bad for a seventy-five-cent comic book (Jean Dillard was upset because she claimed that she had bid more than the high bid, but Harlan hadn't noticed her; I sent her another copy when I got back to New York).

The auction itself raised over twenty thousand dollars. I told Harlan that he shouldn't call Frances at home in North Carolina until the following day, when he was sure that Karl Edward Wagner would be visiting her in case she fainted on hearing how much money was coming her way, as she only anticipated one or two thousand dollars tops.

Harlan, of course, disregarded everything I said and called her that night, but everything worked out fine.

Another time, Harlan was in New York for an autograph signing (he occasionally did one for conventions and award ceremonies such as the Nebulas), and Len Wein and Marv Wolfman and I took him out to the Carnegie Deli (his choice) for sandwiches. (This was around the time that I was editing the science-fiction graphic-novel program for DC that included Harlan's *Outer Limits* script for "Demon with a Glass Hand."

Now, the sandwiches at the Carnegie are huge—really huge—and are quite impossible to finish for any normal person (note: Brian Thomsen has no trouble finishing one of those sandwiches, but he is definitely not a normal person). We had all eaten our fill and were ready to leave when Harlan asked the waitress to wrap up our leftovers.

We wondered why. Perhaps Harlan might be holding on to them for a midnight snack or something.

We four started walking down Broadway to the Times Square subway stop where we would then go our separate ways when Harlan said, "There looks like a customer" and immediately went over to a homeless person and offered him one of the leftover sandwiches.

The person didn't know what to make of Harlan's charity and was immediately suspicious and wouldn't accept the sandwich, so we continued on our way, with Harlan offering a bit of the leftovers to each of the next unfortunates we came across until our Carnegie leavings were all gone.

There's a small convention called PulpCon for people who are interested in pulp magazines, and it is run by longtime fan Rusty Hevelen. I was a guest of honor in 1985, and I enjoyed myself so much that I decided to return the following year.

So in 1986 I called up Rusty and asked him who the guest of honor was going to be.

"Donald A. Wollheim," he replied.

"Great!" I responded. I had known Don since 1933, and we had always gotten along pretty well.

So the convention weekend rolled around, and I got to the airport fairly early as I usually do, found myself a seat in the waiting area, and started to read the *New York Times*. Soon, there came Don—who was not in the best of physical health at the time and walking slowly—followed by his loving wife, Elsie. From behind the cover of my newspaper, I greeted him, "Hi, Donald!"

Don heard my voice, walked over, and peeked behind my *Times*, and said, "Hello, Julie! How are you? What are you doing here?"

I told him that I was on my way to PulpCon in Dayton.

"Well, so are we," he replied. "That's great! Let's sit down and talk."

We had about half an hour before the plane was to leave, so I sat down facing him, with Elsie seated at his right. We kept talking for fifteen or twenty minutes, trading really great old anecdotes about years past.

After about twenty minutes, Elsie interrupted. "Stop! I can't stand this!" she said. "This is all very interesting, but *who are you?*"

"Elsie!" I replied. "Don't you remember thirty-three years ago? In 1953 at the World Science Fiction Convention in Philadelphia? I was getting into an elevator with my wife, you and Donald were there, and I introduced my wife to you and Don, and he introduced you to me and Jean. It was only thirty-three years ago. How come you don't remember?"

Elsie shrugged her shoulders and said, "I just forgot." And we returned to reminiscing.

I didn't realize that at the time Elsie was in the final stages of glaucoma and probably couldn't see me well enough to recognize me.

Don eventually went on to be the guest of honor at the 1988 World Science Fiction Convention in New Orleans, an honor for which I am extremely envious.

• • •

Another particularly memorable moment for me was when I was asked to step in at the last moment for that most gregarious and gracious of after-dinner speakers, the erudite and prolific author (previously known as the know-it-all snot-nosed kid from Brooklyn) Isaac Asimov.

The occasion was a luncheon banquet to celebrate the sixtieth anniversary of *Analog Science Fiction/Science Fact* magazine (formerly known as *Astounding Stories of Super Science.* The big to-do was held at the Explorer's Club, and the attendees were a virtual who's who of New York science fiction and fantasy publishing. Isaac was slated to be the speaker, but unfortunately, had fallen ill and was not able to attend.

Now, to say that there are not that many of us still around who were witnesses to the Golden Age of science fiction is a gross understatement. (I remember being at a fantasy convention where H. P. Lovecraft was a posthumous guest of honor, and I found out that I was the only person present who had met the dear honored guest; likewise I have been at Writers of the Future affairs where I have been the only one to have met L. Ron Hubbard, though that is not usually the case since Jack Williamson usually attends those, and he is even older than me), so rather than try to be more verbal and erudite than the dear Dr. Asimov, I decided to do my Golden Age slide show, and it went over great (I particularly remember getting a few laughs when I revealed what sort of Ph.D. E. E. "Doc" Smith claimed: Doctor of Donuts).

For almost all of the audience, names like Stanley G. Weinbaum, F. Orlen Tremaine, and John W. Campbell and

Harry Bates were akin to George Washington and Abraham Lincoln; important figures of the past, long dead and gone. My slide show put pictures to the names and, for some, made them real.

A few weeks later I received a letter from *Analog's* editor, Stanley Schmidt who referred to me as the perfect replacement for Isaac Asimov.

I took it as a super compliment.

JULIE'S HINTS ON WORKING IN COMICS
DURING THE SILVER AGE . . . AND BEYOND
PART THREE
FINAL THOUGHTS

You can never use too many exclamation points and . . .
BE ORIGINAL!
BE ORIGINAL!!
BE ORIGINAL!!!

I still have an office at DC, and I try to come in at least once a week to touch base with people, make a few calls, and just generally be available. (When word got around that I was retiring, my old boss, Jack Liebowitz, then in his eighties, called me and urged me to do this, advising me that it would keep me young—it has.)

One of the theories around DC (first voiced by comics maven Mark Evanier) is that I am kept on a retainer so that they can bring young editors by to show them what a real editor looks like!

• • •

In 1998, Ed Kramer who runs DragonCon approached me about a certain matter. Previously DragonCon had been the site for certain award ceremonies in comics and science fiction and even fandom, but for reasons too numerous and baroque to explain, the venues for these ceremonies had moved on to other locations. So Ed wanted to start a new award, the problem was simple: What was left? What could it be called?

There were already awards for just about everything covered in the field, including such diverse reasons as acts of charity to first fandom (the Big Heart Award) and best libertarian science fiction novel of the year (the Prometheus Award). What could possibly be left to honor?

I had an idea. What about giving an award for dual achievement—that is, achievement in more than one field, sort of like Thomas Jefferson, president and inventor, or Laurence Olivier, actor and director.

I told them that I thought it was a sound idea.

"Great," he replied, "because I want to call it the Julie! The Julie Award for multiple life achievement!"

I was thrilled!

Imagine, an award named after me! As Harlan Ellison puts it, the only living legend in both comics and science fiction.

I was honored.

Hugo Gernsback had an award named after him ("the Hugo")! I was indeed following in the footsteps of the first man/editor whom I had recognized as being a god on Earth.

The first honoree was to be my longtime friends Ray Bradbury—a worthy candidate indeed, given his successes in fiction, screenwriting, playwrighting, and numerous other fields that include designing a ride for an amusement park. Ray was perfect, and despite the pains of arthritis I agreed to go to DragonCon and present the award to him personally.

Other attendees at the convention and the ceremony, in addition to Ray, were Murphy Anderson, Ray Harryhausen (a boyhood friend of Ray's and himself a very early fan), talented scripter Peter David, and, of course, my good friend Harlan Ellison and his lovely wife, Susan.

When it came time to present the award, I approached the stage with a little assistance and I was surprised to see that there were two Julie Awards present.

Ray was to be the second recipient of the Julie Award.

I, the man of two worlds, the only living legend in comics and science fiction was to be the first recipient of the award that would henceforth bear my name.

. . . and life goes on!

Julie and the "Julie."
(Beth Gwinn)

JUNE 1999 HEROES CONVENTION IN CHARLOTTE, NORTH CAROLINA

Page 6 of the program book bears the one-page article "Why Are We Here? The Answer to One of the Most Provocative Questions of All Time and Space" by Julius Schwartz.

That's right, Julie is an honored guest of the convention, and we are finally beginning to wind down on the book which we hope to see published in about a year—which is why the publisher is urging us to finish and polish.

Next year at this time, Julie will turn eighty-five and what better way to mark the occasion than through the publication of his memoirs.

A lot has happened over the past year.

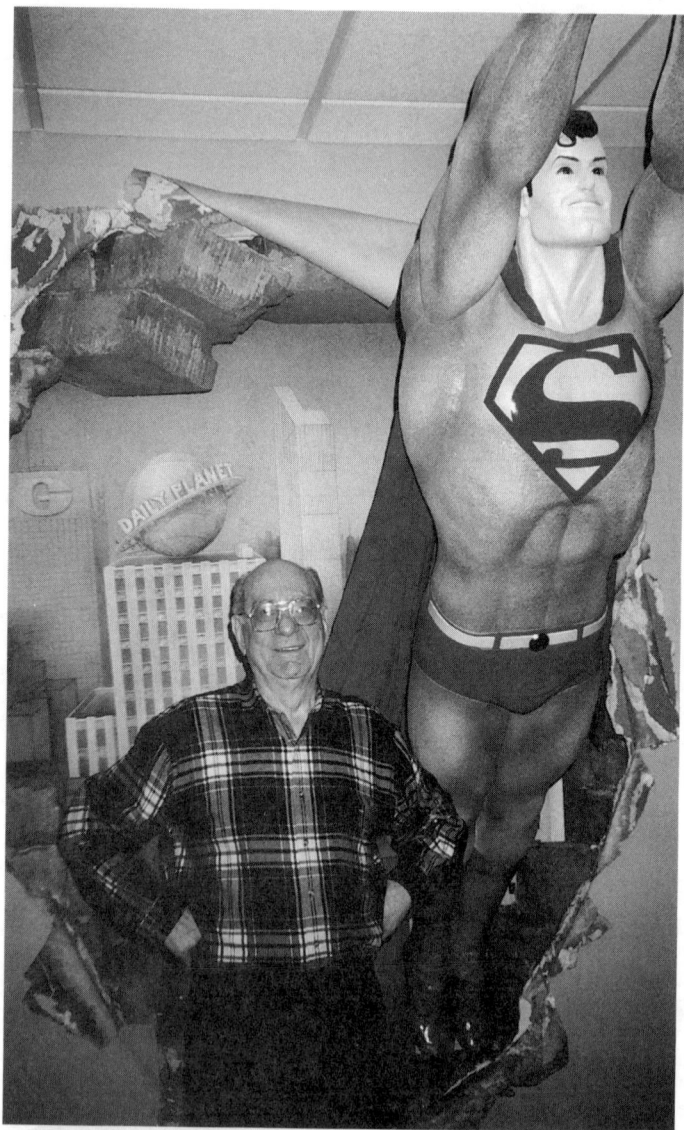

Up, up, and away! (DC Comics)

Some of the friendly faces we saw at San Diego Comic Con are no longer with us. John Broome, Vince Sullivan, and Paul S. Newman have all passed away over the past year (not to mention the credited creators of Batman himself, Bob Kane and Joe Orlando).

Well, enough, about the future and the past—how about the present?

Surprise, surprise! Heroes Convention is filled with card-carrying FoJs (Friends of Julie) among them:

- Harlan "The Great and Wonderful" Ellison
- Dick Giordano, the former editorial director of DC, who retired so that he could spend more time illustrating and inking
- Irwin Hasen, who worked for DC during the Golden Age, prior to cocreating the popular syndicated comic strip *Dondi*
- Shelly Moldoff, who in addition to his own Golden Age work, ghosted Bob Kane's *Batman* for well over a hundred issues
- as well as Mark Waid, Roy Thomas, Keith Giffen, and George Pérez—and even Darth Vader himself, the actor David Prowse

. . . all certifiable friends of Julie.

On Saturday night, a special birthday dinner was held for Julie (number eighty-four) at the Palm Restaurant in Charlotte (the Palm is an age-old uppercrust steak house in New York City that in the past few years has become a franchise, with satellites in the major cities. One of the signature elements of decor in the original restaurant was the illustration-filled walls where the famous artists of the funnies such as Milton Caniff (*Terry and the Pirates*) and Mort Walker (*Beetle Bailey*) drew their famous characters on the steak house's murals. These murals have been copied on the walls of the new restaurants).

A good time was had by all, concluding with the singing of "Happy Birthday" to the guest of honor. (We all plan to come back for number eighty-five next year.) After the festivities, the Charlotte-based Palm was treated to three additions to their murals: a new Dondi original, drawn by Irwin Hasen; a new Batman original by Shelly Moldoff, and a new Bat Lash original by Nick Cardy.

Reproductions are nice, but you can't beat an original.

Julie Schwartz is an original. There will never be another like him, and that's fine because he doesn't plan on going anywhere.

Long live the Man of Two Worlds!

—*Brian M. Thomsen*

FER CHRISSAKES, SCHWARTZ, GET OUTTA MY FACE!

by HARLAN ELLISON

The last thing I remembered was the slam of pain in my chest. Apparently, it had been a heart attack, a stroke, one of those many-named killers that lie in ambush in the body; and I'd felt just an instant of fear before I blacked out and went face-forward. Fear, for that instant, because it had been a coronary thrombosis that had taken my father.

The first thing I saw when I opened my eyes, was Julius Schwartz, crouched over me, shaking me and already talking. At first his voice echoed down a vast, endless corridor to me; indecipherable words carrying no coherent meaning, but only a sense of urgency. And as my senses realigned themselves, as my clubbed persona reified, I smiled. It was a trembly, tiny smile, because I hurt so much; but I smiled, because it was my pal Julie, whom I'd known since I was a pre-teen little kid, who was there trying to bring me back from maybe somewhere like The Other Side. It was good to have a friend who cared that much.

"Get up," he was saying. "Get up! I need you to write a tribute about me for the Con*Stellation 6 programme booke. It doesn't have to be very long, only about six hundred words."

He had me by the shoulders. I couldn't feel my left side. I had the sense that my left leg had gotten twisted under my body when I'd fallen, but I couldn't feel it. There was a huge ash-colored beast sitting on my chest. Breathing was hard. I tried to say, "Julie, help me . . . I think I'm dying . . . call a doctor . . . please let me sit up . . ." but all that came out were a few bubbles of spittle at the corner of my mouth. I realized that the stroke had probably paralyzed everything on the left side, so he couldn't understand what I was trying to say.

He leaned in closer, the light reflecting off his wire-rimmed glasses. "All you have to do is write about how you sent me a letter when you were about ten or eleven, back in the '40s. How I wrote you back and encouraged you. Or when you came up to DC Comics in the '50s, and you saw me in the hall and were too awed by me even to say hello. Or how I wrote you back when you asked for some free art from a *Hawkman* story. You can do it, kid! Just let me help you up and here . . . here's a pen . . . let me put it in your hand . . ."

He got me sitting up, there on the floor. The paper was a DC notepad with a bunch of their superhero characters holding up a DC colophon. And at the top of the page it said: FROM THE ALTAR OF JULIUS SCHWARTZ. He dropped the pad on my lap. I didn't feel it hit. The he jammed the Pilot Fineliner into my right hand, and lifted the hand and dropped it onto the pad.

I'm left handed, Julie, I tried to say; but I guess I only thought it; because I couldn't write, and started to cry. Not much of tears, just a wetness or two that ran down my cheek as I tried to slip back to the floor; but Julie kept me upright, and he tried again to get my cold fingers to hold the pen.

"You can just write about all those dinners we've shared through the years, and how you always try to get DC to pay for them. Or you could talk about how it took you ten, fifteen years, whatever it was, before you wrote that *Batman* script for me. There's a *world* of terrific things we've shared that you could write about. Just sort of a friend-to-friend tribute . . . you know what I mean!"

And I couldn't stop crying, because I hurt so bad, and obviously Julie didn't understand that, so I grasped the pen in my right hand as best I could, with my fist around it like a baby trying to use a Crayola, and with scrawling lines that trembled and didn't match, I scrawled the only tribute I had in me. I scrawled: I LOVE YOU, JULIE.

And then I closed my eyes, and I died.

THE AWARDS, HONORS, AND ACCOLADES OF JULIUS SCHWARTZ

Science Fiction
- Forry Award (1984)
- First Fandom Hall of Fame Award (1986)
- Raymond Z. Gallun Award

Comics Hall of Fame
- *Wizard Magazine* (1993)
- Jack Kirby *(1995)*
- Will Eisner *(1997)*

Comics Lifetime Achievement Award
- Inkpot Award (1981)
- Comic and Fantasy Amateur Press Association Award (1989)

- GEM Award (1991)
- Comic Book Marketplace Award (1997)

Special Comics Awards
- Alley Award (1961)
- Shazam Award (1970)
- Eagle Award (1978)
- Eagle Award (1979)

Multi-achievement Awards
- Jules Verne Award (1984)
- Atlanta Fantasy Fair (1988)
- Chicago Comicdom (1993)
- Julie Award (1998)

THE COMIC BOOK CAMEO APPEARANCES OF JULIUS SCHWARTZ

Action Comics #469, 479 (cover), 517, 533, 569, 571, 575

All-New Collectors' Edition #C-56

Ambush Bug #3

The Batman Family #1, 12

Detective Comics #337, 358, 361, 365, 370, 378–380, 382–383, 400, 453, 465

The Flash (1) #179, 238, 277

Green Lantern (2) #39, 48

The Inferior Five #6

Justice League of America #46, 123–124, 153

Barry (Flash) Allen drops in for a visit, in Flash #179.
(©2000 DC Comics)

Kingdom Come: Collected Edition
Metal Men (1) #15
Mystery in Space #69, 74, 77, 79, 83
The New Teen Titans (2) #13, 48
Secret Hearts #84
The Secret Society of Super-Villains #13
Strange Adventures #53, 67, 77, 82, 109, 113, 136, 140,
    149, 159
Superboy (1) #182
Superman (1) #411
Superman: The Wedding Album #1
The Unexpected #128, 145
Wonder Woman (1) #220, 225
World's Finest Comics #213